Against the Grain

Against the Grain

Khalad Hussain

Cover picture by Nick

To order additional copies of this book, contact:
Xlibris Corporation
0-800-644-6988
www.xlibrispublishing.co.uk
Orders@xlibrispublishing.co.uk
304942

Contents

Dedication

For a long time, I have been conscious that, above all, the Lord has blessed me with a mind that is becoming increasingly knowledgeable. Given that this book is the fruit of that blessing, I hereby give it back to Him. It is His to do with as He pleases, to fulfil His plans for our world and the communities within it and to be glorified in the process.

I also dedicate the book to my parents, for whom I pray that I meet them in the next life; to my children, who helped me to grow up and to my wife, as without her I wouldn't be here.

Stories of Ji

I grew up hearing stories about Ji. These were told mostly in our home and in our village. The stories were told by the many members of my extended family, but especially by my mother. These stories were all I had for the first five or six years of my life because he wasn't there. I could say that he was an unseen presence in our home. He was certainly an influence on everyone including myself.

The stories of Ji were of a good man. Everyone spoke of him with respect and even admiration. Our community was close and talking about others in the village was a popular pastime. At first I wondered who he was. I soon learned two important facts about Ji: he was my father and he was far away in another place called *vilayat*, a Persian term which gave rise to the term *blighty*, meaning England. As a young boy, my horizons only went as far as my village and I had no idea what 'far away' really meant. He was actually Munshi Ji but everyone referred to him as Ji.

Most of the children I played with had their fathers at home. I learned in later life that it was not unusual for fathers in our district to go away to England. They sometimes came home for a visit, but would then return back to this foreign place. Having these men away from their country had many advantages; the money they sent to their family benefited the whole community, even the whole district of Mirpur. No wonder people have come to refer to the area as 'Little England.'

Because of Ji sending us money, we were the first family in our village to build a *pukka*, brick, house. I had so much fun with the builders. They had come from parts of Pakistan I had not even heard of. They would stay for many months and would occasionally go to visit their families. Our village was a bit like their *vilayat*. While they were building our house, we had to feed them two meals a day. I looked forward to all the delicious meals my mum made.

I remember a visit from the police at this time. They came to investigate where we had bought the timber; had we bought it from the 'black market'? All I could see was that they stayed for a while and had a cup of tea or a meal . . . Then they went away. I never did discover the origins of the timber but one thing was for sure: they won't have been satisfied with just drinking tea. In such situations, I discovered later, officials always expect and get *chaa-paani*, something to line their pockets with.

Then, one day Ji came back and stayed. "When was Ji going back to England?" became one of the most frequent topics for the village gossips to chew over. Ji seemed to be above it all. He certainly didn't see the need to conform to the norm or the expectations of the rest of our family or the village. He was of a different mindset. In a community such as ours, being different wasn't always approved of. Although Ji seemed to be turning his back on England, it didn't alter the respect that everyone gave him. He was different.

Whenever I had the courage to ask him, he filled in the details of some of his life's story. For me, learning about his life was instructive and enlightening. As I grew older, the more I understood. I began to see that Ji was a special man. I learned from him that it was fine to be different so long as you were being true to yourself and not a slave to the opinions or customs of others.

Ji was only six months old when his father had died. There was no point in asking how he had died. If I had asked, I'm sure he would have said "He was ill," or "He had a stomach ache." People in our world then rarely knew anything more than this. Many illnesses were a mystery; you were sick and if you recovered, it was God's will. If you didn't recover, this was also God's will.

When he was about eight years old, Ji's mother married again. After this, all he would say was that his life was "very difficult." Apparently, the new husband did not want Ji because he was the son of another. Better to reject him now; who knows how things may turn out to be or how much of a burden he might become. He might be bad luck or he might dishonour the family. Why take such a risk for a boy that is not your own flesh and blood? So the little 'orphan' boy, as Ji was known, lived in whatever house he could find food and a bed for the night. What his mother felt about this was not important. Her priority was to survive as best she could and the customs of their community allowed her to be another's wife, but not to dictate to the new husband, whatever her feelings were. This was how life was and she had to accept it.

When he was considered old enough, Ji was married off to a first cousin-brother's daughter. Given that he was the only son and his father's brother had five sons, he was advised to marry into their family. This was seen as a way of building family alliance with people who would no doubt have their eye on his land. After all, he had as much on his own as they did between the five of them.

They had three daughters. This must have been extremely disappointing for them, given how people relish having boys and commiserate at the birth of girls. Soon after the birth of the third child, Ji's wife died. Again we don't know why or how. Having three girls to look after must have seemed an impossible job for Ji. This was particularly so because he spent many days away from home earning a basic living by transporting goods for people with his donkey. At first this was in pre-partition India and then, after 1947, in our newly formed nation of Pakistan.

One time he came home from one of his long journeys and discovered that his daughters had gone to sleep without eating as there was no food in the house. He was not prepared to allow his children to be neglected, even if they were girls. He decided that getting married again was the only answer. His second wife was also the daughter of a first cousin-brother, one of the other ones. I have no idea how well the new wife looked after the girls, except that in a culture where being a step child, especially a step daughter, has given rise to some horrendous tales of abuse. What we do know is that she failed in her most important role. She not only failed to produce a much-needed son for Ji, she bore no children at all. According to the culture, a woman's main function was (and still is!) to produce lots of children, especially boys. She had obviously failed to deliver. Of course, this was seen as her fault.

According to the culture, Ji now had grounds to divorce her and marry again. However, given the extremely low status for divorced women, Ji would have been under immense pressure to marry another without divorcing her. Her parents had off-loaded their *izzat*, their honour, onto him; they didn't want her back. I grew up hearing people saying that daughters should leave their parental home in a bride's *dholi*, and only return when they die.

So, Ji married Bey. Yes, you've guessed it, she was also a first cousin-brother's daughter. The alliance between him and his first-cousins was well established after these three *rishtays*, marriage relationships. This was especially as he had agreed to stay married to his second wife. She would stay next door to her parents. This way they would look after her but symbolically, her izzat would remain Ji's responsibility. It was also handy for her brothers because they would have a readymade carer for the parents when they reached old age. So it worked well all round.

Hey presto! Bey soon gave birth to me and then, afterwards, my brother. The family must have been in seventh heaven and Bey was a seen as a very special woman married to a very special man. Sadly, my brother did not live long and died through some illness; it must have been God's will. Later, after Ji's return from England, Bey bore two daughters.

Around this time the government decided to build a large dam in the area. This was to provide water to the people who needed it, for themselves and their land. It was also to produce electricity. For some reasons, our area didn't see any benefits, just lots of heartache.

The dam had caused many thousands of people to become displaced. They were encouraged to resettle in other parts of Pakistan, but this was easy to say for the government officials who had little appreciation of what it means to belong to a place and a community. To walk on paths which have been walked by your ancestors for generations or to eat the fruits of the soil which has been in your family for ever or to breathe the local air; these were things they could not understand or appreciate.

The world in which we lived was not used to people moving house as happens in other places. The place you are born is your family's inheritance. It has been there forever and it will go on being there forever. People would be willing to kill for their land. This was part of their whole being. So being told to leave their land and relocate elsewhere in Pakistan would have been an unimaginable concept. The dam had submerged whole villages. They had heard about people becoming *muhajir*, refugees, as a result of the partition of India but now they were being made muhajir by their own government. Would they be welcome in their new place? Who would be living next to them? Whose land would border theirs? Would there be *apney loag*, our people, or foreigners? Would their girls be safe? Would there be schools for their boys? Would they have to be taken to school rather than allowed to walk with their friends as now? And what about the family home and land they were leaving behind? This was their family's heritage. This was where the previous generations were buried, in the village graveyard. What would happen to these graves? What about those buried inside them? Will they still be able to go to heaven on the Day of Judgement? On and on the list of questions went.

People affected by the dam were paid compensation. For poor people, used to surviving from one day to the next, with a few rupees in their pocket, to suddenly be given many thousands of rupees was too much to take in. They didn't know what to do with these large sums of money.

Some thought they might be better off going to England. If you have to leave your home and set up anew somewhere in your own country, why not go a step further and go to another's country? After all, they knew these *gorey loag*, white people, to be decent folk. They were honest people who didn't take bribes. If you deserved something and were able to explain it to them, they would let you have it. Who you were, which *quome* or caste you were, did not matter. You could be king or a servant, they would treat you the same, with respect and decency.

Before this time, there were some isolated people who jumped ship and decided to make a life in England. However, the bulk of the migration from Pakistan began in the 1950s. This was at a time when, soon after independence, people in our new country were looking for work and it just happened that post-war Britain had plenty of such opportunities. There were many jobs which the locals could not or would not do because they were seen as too dirty or menial. There was no such problem for the *Jat* men from our community. No job was too hard for those who had proved their strength in the fields of the Punjab. Nor did they mind doing dirty work as long as the pay was right. Every one pound they saved and sent home could be exchanged for twenty rupees by their family. Compared with the hard living they toiled for in Mirpur, this was wealth indeed.

Word soon got out that someone had decided to use their compensation from the dam construction to go to vilayat. In our world, the hardest thing is to be different, to be the first one to do something courageous. People look to each other to take the initiative. What would people say! Now some brave soul had started the process which others could follow.

People talked about a man, Baba Zaman, from our area who had gone to England a long time ago, before anybody else. He had done so well that he was able to send for others. Apparently, he had persuaded the Queen to give some passports for his relatives. What did he have to do to win favour of one so high and mighty, they wondered. Anyway, he managed to get some passports and give them to his family men. Was this how Ji went to England?

I was about one year old when Ji left us for England. He returned when I was about six years of age. He didn't talk much about his time away other than that he lived in a relative's house. I was to live in the same house myself many years later. He also said that he worked in a factory. He talked about how he used to go to the park and see English people going about in their white t-shirts and shorts.

The only other thing he used to talk about from his five years in England was a visit they had from a man who went by the name of Sirsimon. He had come to find out how the Pakistanis were doing. "He asked us questions, in a strange accent, the way *Gora Sahib* loag talk Urdu. We told him 'No problem,' meaning we were okay. He walked around the house and wanted to see how we lived, where we cooked, slept. He even wanted to see the toilet. He kept saying: *boht khoob, boht khoob*, very good, very good, as he walked around. He also asked a few of the men *theek ho,* OK? One of the men offered him a cup of tea but he declined. We then realised that it wasn't English tea, it was *pukki*, proper, tea, the way we have it; not the way the *goray loag* have it." Later, through research, I was to discover that this Sir Simon was the British Representative in Pakistan. On a visit to the UK, he had been asked to look into the situation of the Pakistani community here. In his report, he pointed out that, knowing the sort of conditions under which people live in the villages in Pakistan, their housing conditions in the U.K. were not as bad as he had feared. He went on to point out that, "on the whole, the Pakistan immigrants are a good lot, well disciplined and respectable. They have a good police record and employers like them." Sir Simon explained that he did not find any evidence of racial discrimination. He felt that the reason some Pakistanis were not getting jobs was more to do with their being unskilled and lacking English and less to do with their colour.

In England, the men (their women did not join them for many years) lived a minimal existence. They would share whatever accommodation they could access. Often this was in houses which had been bought by some pioneer entrepreneur in the family as they did not like paying rent to strangers. They saw this as money down the drain. Outsiders don't always appreciate the overwhelming instinct of our community to keep all their money, property, sons and daughters in the extended family, even if this family is part in Pakistan and part in England. The family ties and loyalties are rarely broken and this is why most Pakistanis marry a first cousin.

In our extended family, there was one such entrepreneur who had bought a house soon after men in our family began to arrive in England. The property had three bedrooms but, in those days, any space that had potential for someone to sleep in was counted as a bedroom. There were men sleeping in the front living room, the back living room and the dining room. The sofas in the living room would double up as beds as would any available floor space. Even the table in the dining room was used at times. In fact, on one occasion, they had someone sleeping on top of it while another slept underneath. The kitchen floor was similarly used when there was a need for such space. Sometime, they would take turns to sleep in the beds. There were times when men would be standing by to get into the bed as quickly as someone got out of it so they could benefit from the bed being warm. Most of the men in our extended family had begun their life in England in this house. This was where Ji lived the five years he was in England. The house was there long enough for me to spend my early days there many years later.

In their new country, the Pakistanis helped the factory owners get even more out of their investments. Having invested their money into machines and buildings, they wanted to keep the factories and foundries open all the time, each and every day of the week. I am told that the three shift system, 6am-2pm, 2pm-10pm and 10pm-6am, would not have existed were it not for the willingness of these immigrant men who were willing to work all the hours God had given them. They worked any shift where they were needed. Some even worked double shifts. The local men did not like to work the night shift and there was a law that prohibited women from working at night! So this became the 'immigrant' shift. In some factories they even managed to establish a two-shift system, a day shift and a night shift, each 12 hours long.

For the Pakistani men, the night shift had many advantages. It paid more; time and half during the week and double over the weekend. Some working the night shift were also happy to have someone sleep in their bed while they were at work. So now even more men were crowded into the houses where they lived, many rented but occasionally bought by the pioneer entrepreneurs in our community. They had no alternative. It was a choice between sleeping outside or in an over-crowded house, owned by a relative. In many towns and cities, they could not get on to the waiting list for a council house, never mind receive one. This was a time when immigrants, especially those who visibly stood out, were not welcome. I am not sure how common signs such as 'No Blacks, no Irish, no dogs' were outside pubs and lodgings but until the 1970s there was no law against it. So landlords were able to turn potential lodgers away because they were the wrong colour. According to an Irish friend, there was a time when the signs simply excluded dogs and the Irish; the word Black was added later when people from the Caribbean and Indo-Pak sub-continent began to arrive.

In those early days of immigration, there was no access to Pakistani-run shops. There was rarely any mention of religion. These men, away from the prying eyes of their families, were more interested in letting their hair down whenever they had the opportunity. However, there was some talk of their struggle with not being able to find halal meat. But they found a way round it by slaughtering the chickens in the back yard. This didn't endear them to their neighbours. It also led to the occasional story in the local papers, alongside stories about overcrowding, as well as a few jokes told by the locals and the comedians in the night clubs; some of them not very pleasant. In a spirit of forgive and forget, it is not worth recording them here.

Life may have been tough but it was better than before. They didn't know much about the white people around them but compared to their own lives in the mother-land, they were now living a life of luxury. They had running water, as much as you needed, for it never ran out. They had a toilet *inside* the house, unlike some people in our community who had an outside toilet. They also could cook by simply turning a knob on the cooker; no having to fetch firewood for the tandoor oven.

Although they had some hot water which came out of a tap, it was never enough, certainly not for the weekly bath for over a dozen men who had been working in dirty factories and foundries. This was when they would resort to the local baths where you paid some money and were able to have plenty of hot water. If you wanted more you could get the key from the *kala*, black, man. One day some enterprising person decided that it was cheaper to pay the man a little more and be allowed to keep the key. So now there was a key hanging up in their kitchen. They worked out a rota for using it.

Soon, the number of Pakistani owned houses increased, usually in the same street or nearby. Slowly but surely the foundations of the community were laid.

The men would save every shilling and send it back home to their families. As new jobs became available they would call for other men in the family, sending them money for the journey. While I was growing up, I recall once the family were distraught because my uncle's camel had been killed by other camels in a fight. This put paid to his ability to earn a living. Soon after, he was called to *vilayat*. Every few years the men would go back to visit their families. They would stay long enough to get married, have children and attend to any family business. While they were away their relatives in England would group together and take care of their factory job so they could return to it afterwards.

One day Ji received a letter from home about some important business he needed to attend to. Had something actually happened? Was it just idle gossip? Perhaps it was a bit of both? He dropped everything and took the next flight back to Pakistan. People tried to persuade him not to go but he wouldn't listen. This was one of the earlier stories I heard about Ji which told me what kind of man he was. Once he had decided on something, no one could persuade him to do otherwise. He possessed great determination.

I heard another story about Ji which gave me further clues as to the type of person he was from a very early age. I learnt about his refusal to tell a lie to save the skin of a close relative who had committed murder. Had Ji done as asked and provided an alibi for the man, he would have been able to stay out of prison. We don't know how this would have affected events; whether this would have prevented the murderer being killed himself by his victim's family when he came back from prison and then his son taking revenge many years later by killing his father's killer. It is obvious, however, that for Ji to refuse such a request from his extended family as a teenager must have taken some courage. It told me about the importance of telling the truth and not lying simply because of convenience.

Under normal circumstances Ji would have returned back to England after a two year stay in Pakistan. However, things didn't work out, I am glad to say. A little while before the maximum time allowed for his stay was up he was injured while racing his bulls in a competition. This sport is one of the ways that the farmers passed the time in between working their farms. When he recovered from his injuries, he packed his suitcase and off to the airport he went.

When he was about to board the plane, the security people stopped him, thinking he was the man they were looking for who was involved in 'black' money. This was an illegal system the men in our community used to send their hard-earned English money back to their families. They kept him in custody for a few days and then let him go, having realised he was the wrong man. He was put on the next flight to London. When he arrived there, the immigration authorities refused to let him in because his two year period had lapsed. Her Majesty's immigration officers are not known for their flexibility or sympathy; they abide by the rules.

Around this time, the situation concerning immigrants had begun to change. Until this point, Pakistanis and other immigrants from the countries of the British Empire were welcome to England; they could come and go as they pleased; they were after all British citizens. Now it had become harder. The government had passed a law which meant the only way to get in was through some sort of a voucher system. People had to be sponsored by an employer before they would be allowed into the country.

Ji tried everything he could to get back to England. He spent a great deal of borrowed money going to different cities and towns across Pakistan, waiting in offices and having to bribe officials at every stage. Occasionally it would be suggested to him that he should go to see such and such influential person to get their *sifaarash*, reference. This would also cost him dearly. None of it was to any avail. He eventually gave up his efforts and accepted that from then on he would no longer be a *vilayati* and that he would somehow have to make a life back in his home country. This too must have been God's will.

Whenever people talked about this, they would say that if Ji hadn't been so stubborn, things would have turned out differently. If he had listened to others' advice, he would never have left England. Mind you, these comments usually came from the same branch of the family whose son had needed the alibi all those years ago. These things are never forgotten.

Ji began to look for alternative ways to earn a living. Sadly there weren't many opportunities available. Certainly not for a *sufaid-poash*, white collar, person that Ji had become. For this kind of person, it would be too beneath him to do labouring jobs; certainly nothing as menial as earning a living with a donkey!

Although Ji had barely attended school for three years, he came across as a more educated person who ought to be in an important job. He had this aura and self-confidence about him, and it earned him respect.

Due to the money coming back from England, a number of Pakistani banks had begun to open branches in our area. Consequently, each bazaar had branches of all the main banks. Each bank had a manager, a cashier and a security guard. The banks also had a *chapraasi*, a trusted messenger and general dogsbody.

The manager usually came from outside the community, from some city in Pakistan. The remaining posts would generally be filled by local people. In a place where there was little other alternative to working on the farms, these were extremely prized job opportunities. So as the local laws of supply and demand would dictate, the jobs would go to people who brought the most influential *sifaarash*. Also, as these banks were competing with each other for foreign currency deposits, they tended to give the jobs to people who had the most relatives and friends in England.

Ji was fortunate enough to land a chapraasi's job in one of the banks. Because this was such a menial job, he would describe himself as a *peon*. I think he must have thought that using a foreign word would somehow make the job sound more respectable. Sadly, even using a foreign word did not make the job any more important than it actually was. He would fetch anything the manager and the cashier needed. He looked after customers, ordering tea for them when they visited the bank. He also visited customers who were unable to get to the bank. An important part of his role was to visit anyone who was known to have money to persuade them to open an account.

As someone with excellent people skills, Ji was particularly good in this role. It didn't matter who a person was, how lowly their position in society, he would speak to them with respect and people treated him similarly. Early on Ji acquired the title *Munshi*. So people would refer to him as *Munshi Sahib*, thus addressing him in a respectful manner.

It was through observing Ji that I learnt how to treat people well. I sensed from his behaviour that everyone, young and old, rich and poor, *jats* and *bazigars*, farmers and artisans, were equal and deserved to be treated with respect. I also learnt about hospitality. He used to drive Bey mad. Whenever he found a traveller staying in the village mosque, he would bring him home and tell Bey to give him the same food as the rest of the family. He used to say, "What good is your praying if you don't look after people in need?"

Ji also taught me about generosity. Whenever someone came to him and asked to borrow money (I am not sure whether they ever paid it back!), he used to put his hand in his pocket and give them whatever he had, saying "I will get more where that came from." One day, we were returning from the local town, which was about two hours walk from our village. In those days, the horse carriage, *tonga*, was the only alternative to walking but which wasn't very attractive on a *kutchi sarak*, unmade road. It was in the middle of a very hot day and it was rare to be travelling at that time. We both had umbrellas. Our heads were also covered with *pernaa*, scarves. We passed a man coming the other way. As usual, we said "Salaam o Alaikum" and he responded with a "Walaikum Salaam". At this point, instead of passing the man by, Ji stopped. He took out his handkerchief and gave it to the man so he could cover his head. The man thanked him and went on his way. I asked him whether he knew the man. He said 'No'. I plucked up the courage to ask how, in that case, he would get his handkerchief back. He said, "Allah will give me another one."

I learned from Ji about the Sikhs and Hindus who had once lived in our village before partition. When partition was announced they had to leave. Muslim women would get onto the rooftops and throw dirty water on them as they passed with their families and belongings. He told me how these despised people were insulted; they would be given water to drink in dirty shoes. He also told me about one particular local man who had so insulted the departing people that he had been given the title *choora*, untouchable. I sensed that Ji felt ashamed about this episode in our history.

There was a woman in our village who had been kidnapped from a camp in India and brought to Pakistan. She was now married to one of my relatives. I used to wonder how she felt about her enforced migration. Did she miss her parents? Was it right to force her to become a Muslim?

The partition in 1947 was a shameful tragedy in the history of the Indian Sub-Continent. Many Muslims travelled to the new state of East and West Pakistan. Likewise, Hindus and Sikhs from the Pakistan areas had to migrate to India. There was a lot of hatred on both sides, stirred up by religious fanatics. More than a million people died. Was it worth it? I have my doubts. I also believe that this is not what the founder of the new country, Mohammed Ali Jinnah, would have wanted. He would not have wanted the carnage that resulted at partition given his belief in religious freedom. Sadly, thirteen months after the birth of Pakistan Mr Jinnah died. The country he helped to found has struggled to become what he had intended.

The state of Kashmir was a mainly Muslim area. It was not part of the British Raj as such, but had the status of "under Dogra rule with protection of the British Crown." At the time of India's partition, the ruler signed an agreement to become a part of India against the wishes of his subjects. The majority would have been happy if the state had kept its independence or had aligned itself with Pakistan, given that most of them were Muslims.

Consequently, the population were up in arms, literally. With the help of Pathan raiders from the North West Frontier of Pakistan, which borders Afghanistan, they managed to gain control of about one third of the state. The area they freed from Indian control became known as Azad Kashmir, meaning free Kashmir, though it was very much under Pakistani control. The area included the district of Mirpur, my family's home.

Soon after the British had left the sub-continent, the Azad Kashmiris wished they hadn't. This was because their new masters were going to build a dam in the area. The locals, having already tasted the integrity and decency of the *goras*, white men, would rather have dealt with them instead of with Pakistan.

Some one hundred years before, the British rulers of India had wanted to dig a canal through the state of Kashmir. The ruler of the state, Partaab Singh, had managed to not only agree excellent terms with the British but also found, to his surprise, that they had delivered on all the terms of the agreement as stated. They could have reneged on the deal; they were powerful enough. Then later, just a few years before they left the area, the British had negotiated a deal with a later ruler of Kashmir, Hari Singh, to build a dam in the area in order to produce electricity. Initially, Hari Singh refused saying:

> *You build a dam in your own area . . . I am the ruler of my people . . . I*
> *do not wish even a single person to be displaced and become homeless. I*
> *do not wish for them to become muhajirs and aliens in another's land.*

Eventually, a deal, extremely favourable to the people affected, was struck so the dam could be built. Amongst the conditions agreed was a clause which said that residents of Mirpur would get completely free electricity and the other districts would be provided it at much reduced rates. Even more critically it was agreed that after fifty years the ownership of the dam would pass from the British to the local people and their own Dogra government. Sadly, the agreement was not to be enacted.

Soon after, Pakistan assumed control of the area. The new government decided to carry on with the plans to build the dam. The new terms were nowhere near as favourable as the old ones. In fact, no one knows what the new agreed terms were (or, indeed, are) for they keep changing. The locals did not get a reduced rate, let alone a free, electricity supply. They had a sense that they would be unlikely to assume ownership of the dam in the future.

The odd one out

One way or another, I gradually realised that Ji was different. He was the odd one out. He would do something if he believed it to be right even if it meant going against the grain.

He managed to convey to me and others that he was educated, important, wealthy, influential and respectable. People would travel miles to ask his opinion or seek his intervention in disputes. Everyone called him *Munshi Sahib*, religious teacher, even though he was not into religiosity. He was much more into demonstrating his faith through his actions.

He was certainly not stuffy; he had a sense of fun. I know, while in England, he had been to the cinema to see The *Ten Commandments*. He also had a small tattoo on the back of his hand. He was cross once when I asked him about it. It was as though he had been found out about being a bit naughty.

We knew Ji was quite political. On some issues, publicly he would choose to go along with others but privately we knew that he believed differently. This was especially the case when it came to the treatment of girls and women. While publicly he did not say much, privately he would always treat my sisters and his wives with decency, barring the occasional loss of temper. This was the same many years later when it came to my wish to marry outside the family. Although he did not want me to marry my English wife, when he saw her he treated her as his own, saying, "She is also someone's daughter."

Those of us who were close to him (and a few others) also knew that *Munshi* he might have been, but he was no angel. In his life there was enough to indicate that he was not perfect; some secrets are best left buried.

We also saw a gentle and loving side to Ji. On many an occasion, I observed him put his hand on his heart after he had shaken it with people as a way of demonstrating respect for them. We lived in a culture where men did not show their emotions. We were, nevertheless, on the receiving end of his affection. I recall once when I had gone to visit them from England, when I was saying goodbye, Ji reached forward and kissed me on my forehead.

The last time that I saw him, when he was very ill and could not manage to get up from his bed to say goodbye, he asked me to bend down to his level. He then kissed me and started to cry. This was probably the only time I had seen him cry. He died soon after.

Only with the passing of the years have I realised that his influence on my life has been enormous. His single-mindedness, his willingness to go against the tide and to stick to his principles have, I believe, rubbed off on me and I thank God for his example in the way he demonstrated qualities such as hospitality, integrity and truth. One of my regrets has been that I was not able to share the news of my faith with him.

My early days

I was born in a village in Dadyal, one of the main areas within Mirpur District in Azad Kashmir.

To say that I was born at home is to state the obvious. There were no hospitals so home birth was normal. There were no doctors for miles. The distance and the cost meant they were definitely a last resort. Some elderly village women will have acted as midwives. It was certainly not a matter for men to concern themselves with. Having played his part, the husband had to let the women folk take care of the pregnant woman who would be described as 'not well.' When the baby arrived, the father would be congratulated if it was a boy and commiserated with if a girl.

I believe my father was away on his travels when I was born. It was not uncommon for him to be away, with his donkey, for six months at a time. Word was sent to him that he was now a proud father who could hold his head up high. He was no longer the man who had to be embarrassed at admitting that he had three daughters.

I have no memories of my father from those early days. Even if he had not gone away to *vilayat* when I was about one year old, he would not have had much to do with me. It was a world where bringing up children was a matter for the mother and other women of the family; the men had to be useful elsewhere.

It was a typical village, like any other in the area. It contained about a dozen households. These were made of local stone. Most would be one-room buildings where the family, whatever its size, would sleep on their *khat* or *charpoy*, a locally-made bed which consists of a wooden frame strung with light rope. If they had the money and space, people would build an adjoining store room and a room for cooking. Otherwise they would use a corner of the main room for these purposes.

Most of the families were *Jat*, farmers. They would have animals to work the land and these were kept in a separate room nearby, to keep the smell away. Of course, there were some like my uncle next door who could not afford to have a separate room, so they shared their one-room house with their animals.

It was a world where everyone had a function and knew their place. *Jats* were the main group. They owned and worked the land. In support, they had the *kammis*, the artisans. The kammi families were generally poorer than the rest and lower status, since they had no land of their own and depended on the *jats*. These were *lohars*, blacksmiths, *darzi*, tailors, *kamhar*, potters, *mistry*, carpenters, *mochee*, cobblers and *naa-ee*, barbers who, as well as cutting hair, had the job of acting as messengers at times of weddings, births and deaths. Everyone lived together as one community. One of the few times we were aware of the differences between the different families was when someone was getting married. People only married within their *quome*, caste, locally or further afield, wherever their family happened to be. It was unheard of for someone to marry outside their *quome*.

It was a simple existence. In homage to Laurie Lee's *Cider with Rosie*, which is the story of his growing up in the Gloucestershire village of Slad, it was a world where life continued as before. There were no roads so people walked everywhere. Our days began and ended according to natural light. The fields around us doubled up as toilets. Women fetched water in clay pitchers from a natural well in a nearby ravine. During the long summer periods, when the well would produce a mere trickle, it was our job as children to go ahead of our mothers and sisters and queue until there was enough water for them to fill their pots. We used to look forward to this job, especially in the middle of the night.

Women were not treated as helpless beings. Instead, they were required to play their full role. Other than being expected to cover their heads with *cheela* scarves, they were not expected to be in *purdah*, veil. Such luxuries were left to richer families whose women sat around doing little, with everything being done by servants.

The whole family would pool their efforts in whatever needed to be done. With the exception of ploughing, which was done by the men, and cooking, which was left up to the women, everything else was gender-neutral. The children and older members of the family did what they could, according to their strength and ability. Before and after school I would look after our animals and help with other chores.

Inter-dependence was at the heart of village life. People were expected to help and be helped by others at times such as death, weddings and harvest times. It was a seven-day existence. There were no days of rest.

We ate home-grown *dhal*, lentils, and the season's vegetables. On special occasions we had chicken. We also knew that once all our chickens had been eaten there wouldn't be any left. These special occasions included those times when we had visitors from afar, the ones who would stay the night. Having walked half a day or longer to get to us, they could hardly be expected to go back on the same day. Red meat was extremely rare; eaten once every few months.

People cooked on wood fires. The wood was collected by people themselves or bought from the travelling wood-man, who went from village to village with his donkey. When I went out with my animals, I would come back with wood I had collected. This earned me some additional praise. Mum thought I was such a good boy.

People would end their days by gathering together in someone's house for conversation. They would often come to our house where there would be a *butti* lantern. The light was just enough to see people's faces. People would talk and listen to stories, short and long, from near and far, from the recent and distant past. It was during one of these times where I learnt how someone had fallen seriously ill and needed to be taken to hospital. He had to be carried on his *khat*. They had sixteen men in the party so they could take turns, four at a time; so heavy was the man who had fallen ill.

Because nothing much happened that was out of the ordinary, anything different was of interest. It would be part of every conversation for many days and months to come. Little events could easily become of major significance. For many years we talked about how they had used a number of camels to help carry a big metal wheel for the *machine* nearby. This was the flour mill where we had our home-grown wheat ground.

When there was no news from anywhere, normal activity would become the focus of conversation. I recall, we talked, for days, about someone taking our buffalo to a village over the hill where she could be 'done.' We as children didn't understand what 'being done' meant; we only knew she had a baby sometime after and began to produce milk for the family. I used to look forward to being given warm milk to drink, just after the milking. This was a reminder of my special status as a boy. I had to sit down to drink the milk because, according to my mum, if you didn't, the milk would go into your legs instead of your stomach. I never saw any of my sisters being given this treatment.

When something significant did happen, people talked about it all the time. It was the focus of everyone's conversation, grateful that they had something of interest to talk about. This could be a birth ("Oh, so and so has six sons now; what a man!" or "They have yet another daughter; poor things, what a shame!"), death, animal stories, being bitten by a snake and so on.

It was a world without music. Occasionally, the artisan families would bring out their musical instruments. This was usually at some auspicious occasion such as the birth of a son or a wedding. The instrument could be a *bansuri* flute, made out of a single hollow shaft of bamboo with six or seven finger holes. I used to love how they moved their fingers over the holes at the same time as blowing into it and did so without looking, as if they had eyes on the tips of their fingers. Sometimes, if it was the younger brother of the bansuri player, we would have the pleasure of listening to a *dholki*, little drum. Even rarer still, we would be entertained with the bagpipes. When this happened, we knew it was a very special occasion indeed. There would be lots of anticipation and a bigger crowd would gather. We would wait and watch the man getting his instrument ready. It would take a few blows before he got going. We watched his neck muscles expand as he blew into his instrument.

People were expected to give money to the musician. Sometime, he would be asked to do a *bail* in the name of someone. I don't know the origin of this word other than wondering whether it is linked to the word 'wail'. The names of the man giving the bail and the one for who he was giving the bail would be called out: "This bail is given by Aslam for his very special friend, Taj". It was always men who gave bails for other men; it would have been inappropriate to have a woman's name called out.

At weddings, when there were lots of people gathered, including some who had travelled many miles from other villages, there would be a competition for bails. People queued up to have their own and their friend's name called out. It was an opportunity to show off your friendships and how wealthy you were.

The only other time I remember music from my childhood was when someone brought a music machine. They would wind it and then put a big black disc on it. When the needle touched the disc, it started singing. I realised many years later that this was a manual record player.

There were no books. Of course, some, not many, families had a Quran. At school we had one textbook for each of the five years—book one for class one and so on. Reading books, other than the set textbooks, was not expected or encouraged. Even if it had been, I have no idea how it would have been possible to get them as there weren't any book shops or libraries. There were no newspapers. Throughout my childhood, I did not know what a newspaper was.

Gossip played a major role in the life of the village. People would hear something and then pass it on, having embroidered it as they saw fit. After a few people had told it, the story looked very different from how it began. It was a culture where people would say one thing in one situation or to one person and another to someone elsewhere.

It was through these conversations that we learnt about the world; the births, deaths, suicides, who had gone to vilayat, who had come back. On rare occasions, we heard about someone being murdered, how much bribe was paid to the police, both by the victim's family and by the accused or his family. When that happened, the police would not know what to do or whose side to take.

As children, we amused ourselves by playing in the open countryside which surrounded us, with whatever toys and games we could make for ourselves. I recall playing *gulli-danda* with two wooden sticks. The danda is longer and the gulli smaller and tapered on both sides so that the ends are conical. The danda is used to strike the gulli and run to a specified point in the marked area. It was simple but it provided many hours of fun for us as children. We could play and keep an eye on our animals at the same time.

We also played a game with seeds or little stones. It was called *sat-khutre*, because it had seven holes, dug into the ground. On one occasion, we used rabbit droppings as seeds but it didn't work as they weren't solid enough. I have since discovered a similar African game called *Awale*, also called *Oware* The aim was to capture more seeds than your opponent. At the end of the game, the player who had captured the most seeds won. It didn't really matter who won or lost; we just enjoyed playing it. I used to love having the seeds in my hand and distributing them, one by one, in the holes. The best part of the game was at the end of the round when you captured your opponent's seeds. We also played with marbles. I used to love potting them and hitting my opponents' marbles with mine.

From a very early age, I knew I was different. This was how my parents wanted me to be. With the exception of an occasional slip-up, I often stood by and watched my friends play and get their clothes dirty. Mind you, many of their clothes were dirty to begin with so it didn't matter much if they got even dirtier. I would be dressed in clean clothes each day and I knew I was expected to keep clean. My mum and sisters would say to visitors with pride, what a good boy I was, explaining, "He never gets his clothes dirty."

Another thing I remember, which kept me apart from my friends, was that I was not allowed to keep a bird like some of the boys. They would particularly keep *buttaira*, quail. They kept it in a pouch and occasionally brought it out to stroke it. They also used to have buttaira-fights, to see whose bird was the bravest. My father thought it was cruel to keep birds imprisoned like this. He used to say that Allah had designed them to be free. Why else would he have given them wings?

Of course, activities such as playing cards were a definite no-no, given their association with gambling. I knew this was something really bad and I should have nothing to do with it. I am glad to say I have made up for it since; thanks to my children I have been able to play many card games. As children, we used to look forward to the annual *mela*, festival. I used to be allowed to go with my older cousins. There were hundreds of men and boys there. I never did understand why the women were not allowed to go to such fun events. So what if someone would see them?

I loved buying a glass of sweet water. They had not yet discovered Coke or Pepsi. I liked watching all the sports like *bini*, a kind of arm wrestling, and stone-lifting. There would be dog and cock fighting. The big events also included ox racing. This was when two oxen were bound together with a wooden yoke on their necks, and they would have a man behind them with a stick. The aim was to see who had the fastest oxen. The roar of the crowd made it so exciting.

Towards the end of the day there would be a *kabaddi* match. This involved two teams of men, standing at either end of a field. They took turns to send one of their team to the other side. He had to touch one of the other side's players, who would be standing in a line, and come back to his own side without being caught. I loved it when, during the chase, the man in front would suddenly duck down, causing the man chasing him to go flying over him. He would then be able to get back to his own side, having earned a point.

In homage to Colm Tóibín's Brooklyn, which was about a young woman leaving her Irish village for America, I presumed that I would live in our family home, knowing everyone, having the same friends and neighbours, the same routines. I thought I would find a job locally and marry a local girl.

In our world we children were expected to grow up and one day suddenly become adults. The concept of a period of *youth* between childhood and adulthood did not exist in our society. The expectation was that one day your elders would decide that you were too old to be a child. You would then be married off to someone in your family, usually a close cousin. As you were growing up, it would slowly become clear who you were likely to marry. We knew that in some cases this had been decided as early as birth. For example, if two children of the opposite sex were born within a close family, their parents may decide that when they were old enough they would be married to each other. The idea was to keep our property and land within the extended family.

Getting married meant that you were a grown-up; you knew it and everyone around you knew it. You would now begin to assume control of your life unless, of course, you were a girl, in which case it would be your husband who would take over your life instead of your father and older brothers. I grew up knowing, as did my elders, that there were quite a few cousins for me to choose from for my marriage.

If you were a girl, once you were married you would leave your own home and go to your husband's house where you would cook, clean and look after him and his elderly parents. But if you were a boy, you stayed in your family home and, with your wife's help, began the process of gradually taking over the household as its head. It became your responsibility to look after your parents (and any unmarried sisters) in their old age, providing for their every need. In return, you would inherit all of the family land and property. Things have changed since; now boys have to share their inheritance with their sisters.

Mine was a very happy childhood. I had everything I needed; food to eat, clothes to wear, shoes on my feet and my own bed to sleep on at night. I was conscious that I had more than most other children around me.

I was a boy. This is not just stating the obvious. It meant something; a great deal in fact. In a family that had many girls, being a boy was certainly something special. I knew from an early age that I was seen as more important than my sisters. I was served before them and given the best of everything I asked for as well as some things I didn't even have to ask for; they were just set aside for me in a taken-for-granted way. So, I experienced none of the deprivations which go with being a part of a large family. As I got older, I realised that being a boy was not just special in our family of girls, boys were better in the wider world around me too.

Much of the time, I enjoyed my 'special' position and its many privileges. But as I got older I began to develop a sense of right and wrong. There were times when I felt uneasy that I should be given such preferential treatment, especially when this happened to be at the expense of my sisters and other girls. What had they done to deserve this second class status, I wondered?

My primary school was about half an hour's walk away. Although education was free, not every child went to school. From a very early age, I knew that education was valued in our family, especially by my father. This was yet again a reminder of the fact that girls were lesser beings than boys. Although ours was not a boys' school in a formal sense, there were no girls attending it. They were expected to stay at home and help with the chores. This would be their apprenticeship in running a home; something they would be expected to do later on. Some would be taught the Quran, in Arabic, by their mothers. Given that ours was a respectable family, my sisters had one better. They were sent to an 'educated' family nearby where they would be taught to memorize the Quran, including some of it 'with meaning'. This meant they would understand the meaning of the Arabic words as compared to just memorising and reciting it in Arabic. Later, I realised that this was a bit of a 'finishing' school for my sisters.

One of the reasons why girls were not educated was because people in our community thought they would misuse their education and write love letters to their boyfriends or read novels, which were seen as lurid literature. I felt sorry for the girls. So whenever they wanted to send one of these letters, I helped to write it for them. I could never understand what all the fuss was about. The letters didn't say anything that was bad in my eyes. I realised later that it was the symbolism that was the key. Just to get a 'letter' from a girl had meaning. It didn't matter what was in it.

One of my sisters seemed to be causing some grief for my parents. In addition to sending letters to boys, she would always be scolded when young men were around. She would deliberately let her *cheela*, scarf, slip off her head so she could show off her long black hair with its ribbon. I remember my Mum telling off a man who kept passing our house for no reason just so he could see and be seen by this particular sister: "If I see you again, we will have your legs broken!"

I started school as early as I was allowed to. I studied very hard and usually got top marks. There was one teacher for the five classes. He had a chair to sit on. The only other item of furniture was the blackboard he wrote on. He would start the lesson and then hand it over to the monitor who would keep an eye on things while the teacher moved to other children. I was the monitor in most of my classes.

We sat on the floor, in the open courtyard. It was very dusty and very hot on summer days. We wrote on our *takhti*, wooden board. We would smear the surface with local clay and write on it with our *qalm*, bamboo pen, and ink. Afterwards, we would wash it in the pond near the school and start again. Some of us had a slate as well which we used for our sums. We would use the chalk we bought from the village shop.

We had two sets of clothes for school. One set was a *kurtha-pyjama*, loose top and trousers for summer months. This was made of thin cotton. In the colder months, we used to wear a slate grey thick cotton, called *malaishia, kameez-shalwar*.

We learnt Urdu. This was when I discovered that this was our national language. It sounded very different from the way we were used to speaking in our normal language. It had many words and phrases which were strange for me. For example, for us the word for ox was *daand*, in Urdu it was *bail*; cow was *gaan* for us and *gaa-ey* in Urdu. Sometimes the words were similar while at other times, different. Even, if they were the same, they sounded different. At times, it was a bit like learning a foreign language. I remember on one occasion my teacher said to me, "I saw your father today. He gave me a *toh-faa*." I and my friends got worried at hearing this. We thought my father had sworn at my teacher. It was much later when my Urdu had become more advanced that I realised that *toh-faa*, meant gift or present. As time went on, my vocabulary developed and I was able to read and write text in Urdu, usually in formal situations and speak my normal 'mother tongue' (it was never written) which I discovered many years later was called *Mirpuri*, from Mirpur, or *Pahari*, of the mountains. It was clear to me from very early on that my mother tongue was not a proper language. It was just words which we should use at home and in family situations, not in the company of anyone important.

We were taught to respect our teachers. We were told they were our spiritual parents and were to be respected in the same way we would respect our own parents. There was an excellent relationship between my father and the school teacher, based on mutual respect. This was not the same for all parents. I recall one parent coming to the school with a hockey stick, threatening to beat the teacher who had spoken wrongly to one of the children. This type of behaviour would have been anathema to my family.

I was a very conscientious pupil. Throughout most my time there, I would be in second position. I was sure the reason I never made it to the top position was because it was given over to another pupil who was a close relative of the teacher. Probably the only time I was a less-than-perfect pupil was when I had a 'stomach ache' on the way to school one morning. As usual, I was walking with the other children from our village; we were never taken to school by our parents. About half way on the journey, I don't know what came over me but I suddenly thought I did not want to go to school. So I decided I had a stomach ache. I put my hand on my stomach and pretended to be in pain. The other children, especially the older ones, advised me to go back home which I did. I had a very sympathetic reception from my mother and my *Nani*, maternal grandmother. They told me to go and lie down, especially as they saw my father coming home. When he arrived home and discovered I had not gone to school, he asked me to accompany him. I dutifully followed. I thought perhaps he was going to take me to the doctor. Instead he walked me to school. I went and joined my class and my father went to speak to my teacher. I never did discover what they had said to each other. Nor did my father say anything to me on our journey. That was the only time ever in my life that I missed school.

At the end of each year at primary school we had to pass an exam to go to the next class. Some did not make it and were stuck in the same class for another year.

After five years at the primary school, I progressed to the secondary school. This was much further away. Most of my fellow pupils from the primary school did not go with me. So their formal education was now at an end.

The journey to the new school took about an hour each way. But since walking was natural, those of us who did it did not think anything of it. At the secondary school, we didn't have to sit on the floor; we had benches. Here I was also exposed to a much wider world. I met boys who came from places I had not heard of. Some of the boys had been to the city and had been to see films. They would talk about film stars to show off; also sing film songs by Noor Jahan and Masood Rana. I remember one song in particular: *jado holi jaye lainda mera nam,* 'when you whisper my name.' I also remember one of my classmates used to go around saying: *Tahadi Izzat Da Sawal hey.* I didn't understand what it meant but I was impressed. Later, I realised that it was the title of a Pakistani film; 'It's a question of your honour.' I was envious of these friends, knowing at the same time that some of them looked down on us as *jungly,* country bumpkin.

At the secondary school, I encountered a range of subjects, whereas at the primary school the focus had been on reading, writing and mathematics. Now we were learning subjects such as geography, history and science. Alongside Urdu, we were expected to learn Farsi (Persian), Arabic and English. The first because it would help us with our Urdu, given the two are closely related; the second so that we could understand the Quran and the third because . . . . I didn't realise then why we were learning English but it became clear later, especially at a personal level.

Initially, I found Farsi the easiest of the new languages. It had many words which were the same as in Urdu, which I had mastered by this time. It also used the same script and the alphabet was very much the same. It helped to learn some of the poetry of Allama Iqbal, the national poet of Pakistan some of whose work was in Farsi. He wrote the famous *Israr-e-khudi*, selflessness:*Khudi ko kar buland itna ke har taqder se pehle Khuda bande se ye poche bata teri raza kia hai* (Elevate your *khudi* to such heights that before every decree, God Himself asks you: "Tell me, what is your wish?")

Next, in terms of ease, was English. Although different from anything I knew, I really liked its structure. Maybe I liked its strangeness. The language which had the least impact on me was Arabic. Although I had come across it when learning the Quran, it had little in it which interested me.

I continued to work hard at my secondary school. Only once I recall 'being given the stick', beaten with a stick on my hand. This was because a few of us had challenged the school rules. I really felt humiliated but for some of my friends this was nothing as they were used to such punishment. In fact, there were one or two who chose to be beaten almost every day. For them this was preferable to doing their homework. In a strange way, I used to admire these boys. I wanted to be like them. I wish I could also 'take the stick' like they could. The 'stick' was not the only punishment; there was the *murgha*, cockerel. This was when the boy being punished would have to crouch on the ground, bend forward with his head well down and bring his hands through from behind his knees until he could grasp his ear lobes. The challenge was to see how long he could stay in that position. Fortunately, I never had to become a *murgha*.

After my father went to vilayat and began sending money back, we became one of the richest families in the village. On the back of the English money, we were the first family in the village to build a brick house. We were quite a generous family too. No one was ever turned away from our house in need of water, food or money.

One way or another, from a very early age, I realised that our family was different from the others. This just added to my own sense of being different. It was to become clear many decades later that the seeds for going against the grain were sown in these early days.

The community had clear rules of right and wrong, based on what was normal. Tradition and concepts such as honour and shame played a major part in the life of the community. There was a saying that there were three things which could offend one's honour: *zan, zar* and *zamin,* meaning women, money and land. However, in reality, the first, 'woman', and the last, land, mattered the most. Just by looking wrongly at a woman of another family could cause offence and lead to major incidents. This was one of the reasons why families were not happy to have daughters. And for those who did have one or more, they would try to marry them off as soon as possible after they became 'women', just in case they did anything to damage one's *izzat,* honour. Marrying them off meant that they were now the responsibility (ownership!) of another family. Their *izzat* would now be transferred from their father and brothers to their husband and his family.

In that environment, it was more important than anything to have one's *izzat* intact. Parents of unmarried older girls would literally lose sleep through worrying in case they got up to no good at night. Death was at times preferable to living with shame. This explained suicide and honour killings. One of my childhood memories is about a woman in a neighbouring village who was caught in bed with a man who was not her husband. That same night she committed suicide by jumping into a well. She was buried, probably in the dark and without a *janaaza,* funeral prayer, in an unmarked grave. The sooner she was erased from collective memory the better, lest she give other girls ideas! The man had to pay no such price for his actions. It was all blamed on her for tempting him. There was no official involvement, no post-mortem. There had been a death for sure, but it was not murder. How could it be; she deserved to die! Someone would have gone to register her death, saying she died naturally, no questions asked. Even if doubts were raised, a few rupees would make them go away.

We never did discover the details. Someone must have caught her and the man together. Someone else or the same person must have told her to jump into the well. What was going through her mind while she was walking from her house? Who pulled her body out? How was she buried? Where was her grave? Did people go to her parents to pay their respects or would that have been seen as rubbing their nose in it?

Our parents advised us to take a different route to school so we did not have to go pass the well where she had died. They knew we boys were a curious bunch. They wanted us to move on from this terrible incident.

So young girls were married off as soon as they had reached womanhood. Usually, this would be done in order of age. The same was true with boys. Although my parents felt it was a shame that they had so many girls, they considered themselves lucky because another closely related family had a bunch of boys. So my sisters' future seemed set. But, something went wrong when it came to marrying them off.

For some reason, my youngest sister was married off first; her older sister was still waiting for her turn. Also, she was married to the older cousin and not his younger brother. I have always thought had things gone according to the usual plan and she had married the younger cousin, her life would have been better. They would have been a better match.

But, given that she was a handful, our parents decided to hand over her *izzat* to her new family. She would soon be taken to *vilayat* as her husband had already been there and was returning soon after getting married.

As I grew up, I realised how people's lives were governed by 'what would everyone say.'. In a culture where everyone lived their lives conscious of the opinions of others, honour and shame had a particular position. Here it was clear that death with honour was preferable to a life of shame.

There was no such thing as 'private' business. People were able to walk in and out of each others' homes. So, people's lives were lived as if they were common property. This kept them in check. They knew that as soon as they stepped out of line, people would find out and tell everyone else. We knew it was normal for people to spend a great deal of their time talking about others' affairs. The phrase 'mind your own business' had little meaning in our community.

The community was also big on hypocrisy. Some things were not talked about publicly, so the suicide was forgotten. People behaved as if it had never happened.

Religion was insignificant. It had little to do with people's regular lives. As a taken-for-granted part of our lives, we were not very conscious of it. There was no getting up every morning and thinking "'I am a Muslim." Mind you, this was also the case in relation to other aspects of our identity. I wasn't aware of who I was other than perhaps being a boy or being from a respectable family.

As I got older, I realised that ours was a 100% Muslim community. For us, our religion, Islam, was synonymous with being Pakistani. It was implicit in the environment which surrounded us; as if it was in the air we breathed. So for me it was as natural as daylight that I would grow up and spend my life as a Pakistani and a Muslim.

My first encounter with religion, like any child, would have been the call to prayer, the *azaan*, being said into my ears when I first arrived into this world. This was said by my father as he was one of the few people who knew the words. He would have said it in Arabic given it was a religious and holy act. This meant that he himself and anyone listening would not have understood what was being said. It goes like this:

> *Allahu Akbar* (God is great)
>
> *Ash-had an la ilaha illa llah* (I testify that there is no deity except for God)
>
> *Ash-hadu anna Muhammadan rasulullah* (I testify that Muhammad is a Messenger of God)
>
> *Hayya 'ala-salatt* (The time for prayer has come)
>
> *Hayya 'ala 'l-falah* (The time for worship has come)
>
> *Al-salatu khayru min an-nawm* (Prayer is better than sleep)
>
> *Allāhu akbar* (God is great)
>
> *La ilaha illallah* (There is no deity except for God)

For girls, this would have been the end of it as far as religion was concerned. But being a boy it meant there was more to come for me. A few months later, I was circumcised. Every boy will have had the same experience, sooner or later. It is conceivable that some children had missed the azaan when they were born and no one would ever know about it. But circumcision was different. It was soon known by everyone which boy hadn't been done and this would then be the subject of everyone's conversation and would put his family under pressure. So, better to do it early and avoid being the subject of such conversation and some amount of shame that went with it. As well as circumcision, my first hair was also shaved as it is seen as unclean. I don't believe this is done for girls.

Most families in the village were not religious. They seldom, if ever prayed. They did not have a copy of the Quran and, if they did, it would be somewhere in the house, wrapped up in a scarf, gathering dust. Perhaps the only bit of religion they practised was fasting during the month of Ramadan. In a world where cooking is done in the open at set times, it was difficult to not fast.

So, had I been one of the other boys in the village, religion would have played little further part in my life. I would have gone through life guided by the culture around me, doing whatever I wanted to, especially if I could get away with it. Then in my old age, I might have turned to *Allah,* bearing in mind that I could soon be facing him so I had better watch my step. I would have begun to say all of my five daily prayers. I would have stopped pretending I was still young by starting to cover my head with a scarf or a hat, and colouring my hair red instead of black. I might even go to Mecca for my *hajj,* pilgrimage, if I could afford that very expensive trip.

But my religious journey began differently. I would follow my father's example. He was quite religious so that is what I aspired to be.

From a very early age, I began to learn to read the Quran in Arabic. This meant I didn't understand what I was reading. At the time, I didn't question it but later I began to wonder what was the point of reading something if you don't understand it. When I finished reading the Quran, our family had a *khatme-Quran* celebration over a special meal. For months after, my parents did not stop talking about it; so special was this occasion for them. Not only was I considered better than many other boys who could not read the Quran, I had finished mine at such an early age.

Because it was holy, those families who a Quran kept it high up in the house. We were told that we mustn't ever have our back to it so if during reading it you had to stop and go somewhere, you would walk sideways.

We also had to make sure that we were clean before touching the Quran, that is, we had done a *wuzu,* ablution. This meant washing our private parts, hands, face and feet according to clearly laid down rules and in the order stipulated. Very early on I remember my father going through all the steps of a wuzu so I wouldn't get anything wrong. He pointed out that, after I have done my *istinja*, washing my private parts which I must do with my left hand, I had to:

1. Wash both hands up to my wrists, between the fingers

2. Wash into my mouth, three times, using my right hand (I knew already that my left hand was unclean. It was only to be used for picking my nose, wiping myself after I had excreted or if I needed to scratch my private bits. I also knew that the left hand must never be used for anything 'good' like shaking hands, giving something to another person, eating or writing. I had seen children used to be smacked if they used their left hand for writing)

3. Sniff water up my nose, three times using my right hand

4. Wash my face, three times from my forehead to the bottom of my chin, and then along the sides up to my ears

5. Wash my right and left arms, up to the elbow, again three times

6. Wipe my head with a wet right hand

7. Wipe the inside of my ears with my little finger, the back of the ears from top to bottom with my thumbs.

8. Wipe the nape and sides of my neck with the back of my wet hands

9. Wash feet, starting with the right one including ankles and between the toes

We were told that our wuzu would become invalid if we broke wind, went to the toilet or touched our private parts. We were also told that if we had been asleep, we must do a new wuzu because "You never know what you might have done with your hands while asleep or what might come out of your body." I realised what this meant when I was a bit older and some of the older village boys explained it to me. The standards of cleanliness were so high that women were expected not to pray during their periods.

I did wonder if Allah hadn't been so fussy about people being clean before they prayed or read their Quran, more of them might have done it. It was sometimes hard to keep track of whether you had done anything which had invalidated your wuzu.

As well as learning to read the Quran, I learnt my daily prayers. This meant five daily prayers at set times; with a set script, in Arabic. The prayers had set movements—bowing, standing, and prostrating. It was explained to me that the prayer times were dictated by the rising and setting of the sun. Because it rose and set at a different time each day our prayers had to be said a few minutes later or earlier than the previous day, depending upon whether it was winter or summer. Later, when a mosque was built, they put up a prayer timetable up so we wouldn't get the times wrong. I wondered what would happen to the prayer if it was a few minutes earlier or later than the correct time; did that not count towards our ticket to *jannat*, heaven?

Just as when reading the Quran, it was necessary to have a valid wuzu before the prayers could be said. Occasionally, I used to say the azaan from the courtyard of the village mosque—the same words which would have been said into my ear at birth. In those days, our mosque did not have a *maulvi*, religious leader. Only the big mosques where Friday prayers were said had maulvis. Little mosques like ours were expected to manage without.

I didn't understand what I was saying in my prayers. Nor did I know why the prayers had to be said in the way they were; standing, folding my arms, bending down or prostrating to do a *sajda*. I never thought of asking and was not told. It seemed a natural thing to do. I was a Muslim, in a Muslim community and this was how Muslims prayed and read their holy book. What is there to ask? It would be a strange question indeed; like asking why day came after night or why trees were green.

After doing the wuzu, I used to feel all clean; for the holy activity I was about to perform. Whether reading the Quran or saying my prayers, it made me feel that I had done something special. It would set me up to live the rest of my life during each day. And it was a good life! More critically, fulfilling my religious duties was religious duties was an important part of my 'being'. It was who I was, following in the footsteps of my father, set apart from many of the other boys. But then we were, as a family, set apart from the rest of the village. We were the Munshi family, after all.

Only a handful of the men in the village went to the mosque, and even they didn't say all of the five prayers. Following local tradition, the women were not expected to go the mosque. Although they were supposed to pray at home, I don't think many of them did, with the possible exception of my Mum and even she did not always say her prayers.

I remember one occasion when one of our old relatives died. The whole village gathered. Message was sent to Siakh where our other relatives lived. They made it just in time before the burial. There were lots of people crying, especially women. A few were wailing very loudly. Some of the crying and wailing seemed to be for effect. Because everyone was gathered, those who were close to the dead man did not want people to think they were not upset at the death. So they would cry when they first arrived at the scene.

The dead man was washed by some of the village men and wrapped in a clean white cloth. The body was placed on a khat, bed. Everyone walked around it to have a look. There was more crying and wailing. Then the khat was picked up by four men, each holding one leg, and taken to the *qabarstan*, graveyard. In the field near the graves the men stood in rows behind the *maulivi*, religious person. The field was full of people—there must have been a few hundred there. The women were watching from the sidelines as they weren't expected to take part in the *janaza*, funeral prayers. I and a few of the other boys were also not expected to join in as we were too young. This meant we could watch all the proceedings.

The maulivi said:

> *It is written that it is the right of a Muslim that when he passes from this world to the next then others in his community should pray janazah prayer for him. We have to do it as a congregation. If no one prays the janazah prayer then everyone would be considered sinful in the sight of Allah. But, if some of the people pray the janazah prayer then the whole community is saved from the anger of the Almighty God even though the reward will only be given to the participants only.*

After reciting some Arabic which made him sound really holy, he turned to address all the people, standing in rows behind him:

> *Make sure your lines are straight.*

> *There are four takbirs or Allahu-akbar or God is Great . . .*

I will say "Allahu-akbar" and raise my hands up to the shoulder level
with fingers stretching to the earlobes and you must do the same. Then
I will fold my hands on my chest, right hand over the left.

Then you can recite.

He asked everyone to say Bismillah hir-rahma nir-raheem. Everyone
knew these Arabic words because, as Muslims, they were used to saying
them whenever they began to do almost anything. He also asked them
to recite surah Fatihah, which most of them should have known as it was
the part of the Quran read out whenever someone dies and you visit
their family to give your commiserations.

Without Surah Fatihah, we have been told that no prayer is valid.

Then I will say the second takbir and you should follow by saying the
same; same with the third and the fourth takbirs.

After the fourth takbir, I will say "Assalamu 'alaykum wa rahmatul-lah"
turning my face to the right first and then to the left; and you should
do the same. (As if to make sure everyone understood their right
and left, he turned his head as he spoke)

I remember thinking it was a good idea that people doing the janaza
prayer did not have to go down to the ground and touch it with their
nose because the field they were in had just been harvested and would
have scratched them.

After the prayer, the body was lowered in the grave which had been dug
by some low *quome*, status, people. We children couldn't get very close this
time but we had seen the dead man early on when everyone was walking
by him to have one last look. After lowering the body into the grave, the
grave diggers filled the grave up with the soil. A few months later, the
dead man's family arranged for the grave to be made *pukka*, proper. It
was built up with bricks and a headstone marked with his name, the date
he had died and a prayer, in Arabic, to help him in the next life.

For the next four days, there would be intensive reading of the Quran, in
Arabic. On the evening of the fourth day, there would be a gathering over
a meal, called a *khatam*, meaning finish. There would be a maulvi present.
He would ask how many Qurans had been finished. The more the better.
This could be any number including part-finished. For example, the

family might say sixteen Qurans and ten *separay*, chapters. This would then be presented to Allah who would be asked to accept them and count them in favour of the deceased, especially on the Day of Judgement when his good and bad deeds were to be counted up to see whether he qualified for heaven or hell. I recall once being invited to attend such a khatam with my class fellows at secondary school. The message had been sent to our school with an open invitation to any of the boys who had learnt to read the Quran. After school, we went to the family's home near the school and read as much of the Quran as we could between us, receiving nice food at the end. Of course, we would also be doing a *naiki*, good work, which would help us in the eyes of Allah. I remember this especially as it happened to be the day when a letter had been sent to us from England saying that I would be going there soon. It was my duty to pop into the post office to enquire about such letters for our village.

A similar *khatam* would take place on the evening of the fortieth day when there would be reading of the Quran and lots of nice food. It was called *chaaleeswan*, fortieth. This was usually bigger than the *chautha*, the fourth. This would then be followed up with an annual *khatam*, held on the day of the death or burial.

Everyone looked forward to the *khatams* because the family provided the best food possible for everyone who attended. Some even incurred debt to meet this expense. It was a question of their *izzat*. They knew that people would talk about the event forever if the catering had been of low standard.

Then life would get back to normal. People would begin to slowly forget the deceased, except on a Thursday evening. This was when most families would ask the man of the house to pray over some food and water and bless the spirits of those who had died from that household. As children, we were told that their spirits would come back on that evening and wait around to see if anyone remembered them. If this was the case then they would return happy, otherwise they would be miserable and probably think badly of their families.

People who had not made it to the funeral would visit the family and pray quietly. They would lift their hands up and move their lips as if they were reciting *Fatihah*, the first chapter of the Quran. But many would just be pretending to pray. It's highly unlikely that people who were not in the habit of saying their daily prayers would know their *Fatihah*.

When I was a bit older, I also began to fast during the month of Ramadan. It meant having lots to eat at dawn and then no food or drink all day until sunset. In some ways, this was a rite of passage. As kids we used to compete with each other to see how many fasts we could keep. We also used to look forward to the festival of *Eid* at the end of Ramadan. We referred to this as the little *Eid*. A couple of months later we had the big *Eid*. This was when people sacrificed goats and sheep. For us children, both *Eid*s were an exciting time. We used to wear our newest clothes, go to everyone's houses and eat until we could not eat anymore.

For both Eids, there was a big build-up. When the day came everyone celebrated them. Occasionally, fairs were organised for the community, especially children. So one way or another, it was a great occasion.

The only other religious activity we looked forward to was the weekly Friday prayer, in which more people participated than in the rest of the week's 35 prayers. These were usually said in a *jumma masjid*, larger gathering mosque. We would also get out of school early for this.

Later, I learnt about *pirs*, saints. Set apart from our village was a group of houses where the pir families lived. They were some sort of holy families. Whenever we visited them we had to sit at a lower level than them. They would be sitting on their *khat* or *charpoy* bed as usual and sometimes on a chair. But my mum or sisters used to turn the bed upside down and then sit on it; almost touching the ground. I never did learn whether it was out of respect to them or their ancestors. We as children certainly couldn't see anything holy about these pirs.

Near their houses was a *khanqah*. This was where the previous generations of pirs were buried. Sometimes, people used to go there so they could be healed. This was mainly the uneducated people of the village. As children we used to love going to the khanqah because people used to distribute sweets and other nice food as a sacrifice.

In our family, it was always my mum and sisters who went to the khanqah; my father didn't believe in pirs. He tolerated them and showed them respect but never went out of his way to go to the khanqah. He said it wasn't proper Islam to do such things.

I remember once I was given a *taweez*, amulet, after I had been ill for a few days. There was a belief in our culture that if you have a beautiful child and someone admires him this could cast a *nazar*, the 'look' or evil eye, on the child. So a comment such as "Isn't he clever?" or "What a beautiful boy!" could actually cause the opposite to happen. The taweez would act as protection against such *nazar.*

The taweez was a tiny piece of paper that one of the pir ladies gave to my mum. She wrapped it in a bit of cloth and rolled it in a tiny ball, putting it on a string so I could wear it around my neck. It didn't last long. As soon as my father discovered it, it had to come off. She had also been told to put some *surma,* black powder, in my eyes to cast off evil spirits for whom the taweez had not done the job. He said, "There is no mention in the Quran of such ignorant practices. If your child is ill then take him to the doctor." She did as she was told. After this I did not ever have to wear a taweez or have surma put in my eyes.

Other than the occasional bit of fun, it was very clear from those early days that my religion was about 'doing.' The more you 'did' the more likely you were to get into heaven; more prayers, more fasts, more reading of the Quran.

World beyond the village

We as children had little exposure to, or knowledge of, the world beyond our village. Some of the men had seen what lay beyond our immediate environment. Previously, this would have been in different areas of the British India and other parts of the Empire. For example, one of my grandfathers had been to Sydney, Australia on the ships and his younger brother had been to Egypt.

However near or far the men went (it was always men who went, leaving the women at home), they would always return home to get married, have children or sort out their family business. I guess this is what they expected to happen when the men went to England. They were expected to go there for short periods in order to earn and save money through whatever work they could find there. But, as we came to find out, this was just a myth, the 'myth of return.' People intended to return but rarely managed it, and so the community put down its roots in England.

Around this time, many of the men who had come to England on their own had begun to call their sons to join them. Some would also, if they could, take along sons of relatives. I was to be such a child, given that my parents had concluded that they would not be able to give me much of a future in the village.

Because lots of my friends were going, I hoped I would also go one day. I know my father had reservations about sending me to England. One of the reasons for this was that at the time it was known that people could get a job in England without qualifications. He thought this would happen to me and I would end up in some factory job, which he did not want for me. But he had few other options. The whole community was sending their sons to England. If this could not be done legally then any means would do. The only person who tried to persuade my father not to send me away was one of my secondary school teachers. But as it turned out, he had other motives.

There was a man in our extended family, by the name of Afsar, who was some sort of cousin. He agreed to call me to England alongside his wife. It was either a major favour to us or a favour being returned by his family. In order to travel to England, I had to get a visa. I didn't know what this meant but I knew it was very important.

Before going, I was coached. I was told what to say. There was a local man who was called an *agent*. He knew what was what. I was told to tell the visa people my name, my parents' name, the school I went to, names of my brothers and sisters. I remember thinking this was very strange because the answers I was told to give were all wrong. I just didn't understand. But it was made clear to me that I didn't need to understand. All I had to do was to give the 'right' answers.

I also had to learn about something called dateofbirth. "When they ask you, 'What is your dateofbirth?' say . . . ." I was given a date, month and year. I had to memorise it so I did not get it wrong. What did it all mean?

I wrote it all down so I could practice what I was going to say. I used to have the script in my pocket. As well as what I had been told, I filled in a few details of my own such as how long it took to go to school, the primary school I had gone to before the secondary I was at now, the friends I had and the names of the teachers at both my schools. I didn't have to worry about what subjects I had studied at my new school since they would be the same as my real school.

My 'mother', Afsar's wife, was also prepared for her interview. She was told to keep her answers simple. Apparently, we had few relatives and they had very few children. I heard the 'agent' man say, "You have to be careful. We don't want them to start making links with other members of your family who have already gone to vilayat or might follow later."

I wrote some of the script in Urdu and some in English. I underlined some of the really important bits. I found the best place to learn it was when I was out looking after my goats. Walking around, I would find a big stone to sit on and look through the script. I used to get my friends to ask me questions about my new identity as a bit of a rehearsal.

Going for my visa was a big adventure for me. It gave me an opportunity to go to the big city. One of my memories from that trip is seeing all the electricity pylons as our bus travelled across the plains of the Punjab. They looked as if they were holding hands with each other.

Generally, our culture has a very relaxed attitude towards time. There are situations where it doesn't have to be specific to the hour. For example, if visiting someone in their home, you might send a message to say you are coming without saying what time. It is really not of any consequence what time you show up. You will probably try to avoid meal times unless, of course, you were invited for a meal. You will stay for a reasonable amount of time before leaving. You wouldn't stay too little nor would you wish to overstay your welcome. It all depends on the occasion. Each occasion has rules, not written; nothing as formal as that, but rules nevertheless.

Given this was an important occasion, we did not want to be late for the visa interview. We had been told that the English were very particular about time, down to the last minute. If the interview was at 2 o' clock then that is when they will see us. Not before and if we are late then we will miss the opportunity and might have to wait a long time for another appointment. We certainly did not want to be late for this important occasion, so it was decided that we should go the day before and stay at a hotel. This was the famous Nasim Hotel, in Raja Bazaar. Apparently, all the *vilayat*-bound people from our area stayed here so the staff knew the names of our villages, who was related to whom, who had gone to *vilayat* and their stories. The staff knew our family because my father had stayed at the hotel during all those many visits to the British Embassy while he was trying to persuade them that they should give him another chance to go to vilayat. When he discovered who I was and why we were there, I remember the man who worked at the hotel saying something like, "At least this way *chacha* will have his son go; it wasn't meant to be for him to go back." In our culture, if you are referring to someone older than yourself, you call them *chacha,* uncle, or *bhai,* brother. It is disrespectful to call them by their name. Even if you did have to use their name, you would add a *ji* or *sahib* at the end.

During the evening at the hotel our agent came to see us. He helped to prepare me and my aunt, Afsar's wife, for the interview. She was supposed to be my step-mother.

After our dinner, I did not want to go to sleep. Back in the village, there would not be much to do now, in the dark. But not here. It seemed as if there was no end to the day. Everywhere, electric lights came on and life continued, just as if it was daytime. Opposite the hotel, I remember a big sign which said *Coke adds life to Pindi.* Later, I was to discover that this was reference to a sugary drink that came in bottles.

I stood at the balcony watching everyone going about their business. Even when I did go to sleep, I knew that life was carrying on outside. Then, in the morning, I was woken very early. I remember a man shouting outside our room, *akhbar-ay, akhbar-ay.* It was explained that he was selling *akhbar,* newspapers. I looked out and saw people busying themselves. Had they stopped at all in the night, I wondered?

At the passport place, I remember being interviewed by a brown *gori,* a brown 'white', lady or *memsahib,* which is how English women were referred to. She wore a very tight suit. You could see her legs. I don't think I had seen a woman's bare legs before, maybe my mum's by accident. She also wore nothing to cover her head and her hair looked as if it had been cut, just like a man's. She spoke English. Although I understood much of what she was saying and could probably have replied to her in her language as I had been learning it for three years, I had been advised to speak my own language. They thought it was safer this way. So everything the brown *gori* said was repeated, in Urdu, by a Pakistani man who was sitting there next to her. Equally, everything we said, he would put into English for her. It is possible that the man had been given a bribe by the agent to make sure everything went smoothly in our favour.

I did a good job. I gave all the right answers. However, I was surprised, almost disappointed, they did not ask me about my dateofbirth. One thing I did learn from this experience was that I had the ability to tell lies. I knew I could pretend to be someone I was not. I would have felt guilty doing it but I knew I had the backing of my family. They had told me to do it and I knew it was in a good cause and others were also doing it. But from time to time I did wonder whether a lie is always a lie, whatever the circumstances!

It did not come as a surprise to my school friends that I was going to *vilayat*. Most of them were headed there too. Many of them were just going through the motions attending school. They knew that once in England they would not need education since jobs were aplenty. They would have a choice of jobs with good pay and would soon be back, as a *vilayati*, with lots of money, to get married. There were also stories about getting paid even when you didn't work. Apparently, all you had to do was to go to the government's office once a week. Or was it the Queen's office; we didn't know for sure. But either way, you could collect your money. What sort of place is it where you get paid for doing nothing? We knew in our world people had to work all day, with a little break for food, before they would get their *mazdoori*, pay.

As soon as I had my visa, I became the subject of everyone's conversation.

They spoke about nothing else; when I would go, how I would travel, who would go with me to where we caught the bus so they could help carry the luggage, who would go to the airport, how long this part of the journey would take . . . On and on they would go, everything repeated hundreds of times, some of it by the same person.

Someone would then start talking about my destination, a place none of them had ever been to but knew everything about. Some of it had some truth in it while the rest was made up. They would talk about a Pakistani man, or was it a Mirpuri, who had fought, or wrestled, a white man and won. Someone would chip in that it was, a *habshi*, a *sheedi*, black man, who had won a boxing match and was now the champion of the world. He had become a Muslim but the English people still called him by his other name which was something like Kasees Klay. Didn't the Queen give him his medal? What a strange world I was going to, where a *gori*, white woman, would give a medal to a *sheedi*. Women didn't mind shaking hands with men in that culture. But would she shake the hand of one so dark, only Allah knows!

Someone would then chip in, "Isn't it dark all the time in *vilayat*? You never see the sun." At this point they would turn to my father. After all, he was the authority, having been there. The floor was his now. He would tell us that, yes, indeed, it was dark as the sun never came out. The conversation would move on to the fact that you could turn on the light simply by touching a button. We as kids used to think that this meant that it was possible for a human being to switch the sun on and off. After all, we were talking about the land of the *gorays*; there was nothing beyond them!

If there were any who had been to *vilayat,* they would wait their turn to enter the conversation with their contribution. It had to be just at the right time in order to get the maximum effect. Now everyone would be quiet and turn towards them. They had the floor to themselves. They would speak as if they were the only expert, not just in this conversation, but in the whole world. They were in a position to say anything. If anyone interrupted, they would say, "What do you know about it? You've never been there like I have." They made it all sound as if it was the truth. They could embroider the story if they wanted to, to make it a bit more interesting. In fact, they were under pressure to do so. People need a bit of excitement now and then. How else to get through village life?

People gave me messages for their loved ones, whom they hadn't seen or heard from for many years. The nearest phone was a day's journey in Dadyal. Mind you, they couldn't have phoned anyway as their relatives in England did not have phones in their houses.

People said, "Say to so and so when you see them that the buffalo has given birth and we now have plenty of milk in the house. We have more than we need so we give to so and so whose buffalo has stopped producing milk, or has died, or has been sold . . ." or "Send money because my house has fallen down, or I need to marry the daughter off . . . and give her dowry, or buy a new plough or ox". On and on the messages would go!

Occasionally, they would be told to be quiet. My father, occasionally my mother, would remind people that I was a mere child and would not be able to remember it all. This was their cue to start talking about letters. They would say they have asked so and so to write them a letter but he is playing hard to get, he is always busy or he has a headache. They would hope that my father would acknowledge their plight and offer to write their letter. This would give them an excuse to come back during the day so he could see what he was writing. He said the lantern light wasn't enough. This would also give people something to do, to pass the time, to come and have another cup of tea at our house and sit around for a good old natter.

I also began to write letters for people. There was an established format so it was easy. I would make a start, write the first few sentences and then ask them to tell me what they wanted me to write. Usually, it was two or three things of substance. I would then write the last few sentences. I wrote in Urdu instead of the local dialect. Most likely, the letter would have to be read to the person receiving it in England as many of the men there had not gone to school and could not read Urdu. They knew who in their community could read so, on a weekend, they would visit him and hear the letter being read. They would all hear it; privacy was unheard of in such situations.

As well as letters, people going to *vilayat* were expected to take gifts for people from their loved ones. It could be anything; clothes, shoes, a bag of grain from the recent harvest so their son could get it turned into flour and make *chapatti*, whole-wheat flat bread. What a way to be reminded of their home!

I remember someone turned up with butter for me to take to their relative in England. Well, it was homemade! Another turned up with tobacco. This was before the time when drug smuggling became a problem. After they had gone, my parents said they would throw them away. "If someone asks, say you put it down somewhere and forgot to pick it up." My father was muttering away to himself. He gave me the impression in these situations that he thought he was above people around him; he had different, higher, standards.

During all the time my family was busy making the arrangements to send me to a foreign land, no one asked me how I felt about it all. Did I want to go away from my village to a village in another country, or would it be a big town or city? How was I going to cope without the love of my family and community? Perhaps, more importantly, how was I going to manage without my mummy being there, before and after school and all the many other times? I so looked forward to coming home to her after school.

The focus seemed to be on doing the right thing. Everyone was sending their sons away. I was lucky to find a family who had a 'passport son' of my age. I would have a better future where I was going. The rest was not important.

When the time came to go to England, my father took me to Islamabad Airport, which was a day's journey from our village. The whole village gathered at our house to say goodbye to me. The women all kissed me and the men hugged me. This was no ordinary hug but one for long journeys. You start by hugging the man on the right, then left, then right again. You then shake hands. For young children, the etiquette demanded that they would each come to me and lower their head in front of me for me to put my hand on it, very gently. I had learnt that it was important not to forget anyone in the process; otherwise, they would take offence and probably talk about it forever.

We left with most of the village walking with us. Someone carried my suitcase so my father didn't have to. As we got further from the village, the people walking with us became fewer. They would now get back to their normal duties. Eventually, our party was just me and my father.

After about an hour of our slow walk, we reached a place after which our path would be downhill and I would not be able to see our village. We knew that all the people who we had left behind were waiting to see me for the last time. So, as was the practice, I took out my white *pernaa*, scarf, turned to face our village and waived it in the air a few times. This was my final farewell.

We then walked a bit further before catching a *tonga*, horse carriage, to Dadyal. From here we caught a bus to Mirpur and then another bus to Rawalpindi, passing by the new Mangla Dam.

We booked in at Nasim Hotel, as before. After checking in we went to buy some 'landi kottal' clothes for me to wear. It was explained that in *vilayat* they don't wear *kameez shalwar*, baggy pants and long outer shirt, the clothes we wore in Pakistan. Later I discovered that the 'new' clothes bought for me were second hand western style clothes which had been smuggled into a town called Landi Kottal, near the border between Pakistan and Afghanistan.

Sometime in the evening, the agent man who had arranged my visa came to see us to check everything was okay. My father told me that he had come with my aeroplane ticket and, of course, for his final payment.

In the morning, we travelled by car to the airport. There were a lot of cars queuing nearby the hotel. I think they knew where the customers were. At the airport, my father paid the driver.

We walked to a desk with a man behind it. He looked like a policeman, with his uniform. My father gave him my passport. He checked it and then said to us, "It's okay." My father hugged me. It was many more than the usual three hugs, ending with one long one. He also kissed me. Although men in our community did not kiss, this was an exception.

He told me to go. I walked through the glass doors, into the airport. When I got to the other side, I turned to look behind me, to see my father one more time. The door had closed but I could still see him through the glass. This was it for the next eight years. A new chapter of my life was about to unfold.

But it nearly didn't happen.

I remember our plane stopped soon after. I think we were still in Pakistan. I followed everyone who was getting off the plane. I then sat in a cubicle, somewhere at the airport. Goodness knows what I was expecting! After some time, I was found and put back on the plane. After take-off the man sitting next to me said that he had alerted the airline staff that I was missing and they had then gone to look for me. Apparently, my father had asked him to look after me on the journey. I don't know what his name was or the village he had come from. The only thing I remember about him was that his face was covered with the after-effects of chicken pox. What would have happened if they had left me sitting in that cubicle?

England, my land of hope and dreams

I left behind my mono-cultural, mono-religious, tradition-bound and simple world and came into a diverse, technology-based world with roads, television, music and much more besides.

Once in England, I learnt to stand on my own feet. I had been brought up in a loving and secure world where I felt safe amongst people I knew and trusted. I was used to having all my needs met by my family. It was a culture where children were children and adults made all the decisions. I never needed to make any decisions of my own. Now, it had all changed. I had to make all my own decisions, to survive in a foreign place. I had to decide which school to go to, how hard to study, how to spend my leisure time, how to earn pocket money . . . The list went on.

Before I left my birthplace no one sat me down to talk me through what a momentous step I was about to take by going to a world far away. No one reminded me that when I arrived in my new country, my Mum and Dad would not be there.

When the plane arrived, there was a van, which they called a mini-bus, waiting for us. They had hired it from a Pakistani man in the town, called Aziz. During the journey, I gathered from the conversation that he used to work in a factory but now spent most of his time with his vehicle going to and from the airport, transporting his countrymen on their way to and from Pakistan.

It quickly dawned on me that the world around me had suddenly changed. I was living with relatives I barely knew. I had to get used to my new identity. I was still Khalad in the family but as soon as I was talking to outsiders, I had to use that other person's name which was written on my passport. This was especially if there were white people around. "You never know who might tell the government and we will all be in trouble and sent back." After a while I got used to it. Whenever I was speaking in Mirpuri, I would be my real self, as I would be speaking to *apney loag, our* own people, but when I was speaking in English, I would use my new name, as now I was invariably in the presence of *gorey loag*, white people.

The family who brought me to England provided shelter, food and some basic clothes; the rest was up to me. This 'sink or swim' situation taught me to be independent—both of mind and in action. The significance of this was to become clear many years later.

I liked living in our house. This was the same house where Ji had spent five years of his life in England. I used to imagine him being there with me now. This is how he would become an imaginary presence in my life, right up until his death and sometimes even beyond that. Whenever I did something or said something, I used to try to see it from his perspective. He would often agree with me. It was easy. All I had to do was to think to myself, "If he were here and he had all my understanding, of course, he would say or do the same thing." This even included things with which in real life he disagreed. Even then, I would think to myself, "If he had had my journey and its experiences he would be doing what I am doing." So life was simple!

I had my own room. It was quite a small room, with a small bed which I used to sleep on at night and sit on during the day to read or do my homework.

I especially liked our indoor toilet. We did not have to go to the fields like in Pakistan. It was different from the toilets I had seen in Nasim Hotel in Rawalpindi. With this one, we did not have to squat; we could sit on the seat. Afterwards, we did not have to use stones or even water. We had toilet paper; Izal brand. Although, it was quite a scratchy paper, it seemed a lot better than stones or bits of soil. Occasionally, we used newspapers as toilet paper to save money.

The house also had a bath, with hot water. But I soon remembered the public baths Ji used to talk about. Whenever I could afford it, I would go there and have much more hot water than at home. The *kala*, black, man was still there.

We lived near some gas towers which went up and down. I remember on one occasion there was a big gathering of white people who looked very black. They were miners who were picketing the gas works during their strike in 1972.

A couple of months after arriving in England, I was given a place in a school. It was a language centre where all the newly arrived immigrant children went. I was there for two terms.

The first few weeks I struggled with the cold weather. I particularly did not like the snow. I kept slipping everywhere. The people I was living with advised me to keep my pyjamas under my clothes. Although, this did provide me extra protection against the cold, I stopped wearing them after a couple of days. I didn't like my friends laughing at me as it made me look fat.

At school I experienced, for the first time, things like school dinners, having girls in my classes and going swimming. We were taken on trips to the zoo. Seeing all the caged birds and animals made me wonder what my father would say, given his views on taking creatures out of their natural habitat. We were also shown what a library was and were taken to one near the school.

While at school, I kept getting into fights. "You are a very angry boy," said one of my teachers. "What are you angry about?" I wanted to tell her that I was angry about not having my Mum waiting for me at home, after school. I was angry about not having her cook my meals. I also missed being special; I was just one of many in the house where I lived.

But I could not tell my teacher any of this. I had been told that I must never tell white people about my real identity. Whenever I meet them, I must remember that I am the person it says I am on my passport. I must forget my real name. At first, this upset me very much. I really liked my name; I was given it by my uncle.

The teachers at the school were generally very nice. There was only one who wasn't. When we were sitting in rows with our desks in front of us, he used to tell us to look ahead. He would then walk behind us. He would pick on one or two of us and slap us on the back of our heads. We never knew who he was going to pick on. I really hated it. As he walked behind me, I could almost feel his hand landing on the back of my head. I decided to get my own back and came up with an idea. It was a bit naughty but I thought he deserved it.

One day, as usual, he was walking behind us. I was sitting there at my desk, ready with my pencil in my hand. He picked on me. As he slapped me I let my head suddenly go forward and down. I pretended that the pencil in my hand had poked me in the eye. So, I started to rub the eye. I wouldn't stop. After rubbing it for a few minutes, of course, it had gone red. I pretended that I couldn't see through it properly. Everyone in the class stopped their work and gathered around me. The teacher didn't know what to do. The smarmy look on his face had disappeared for sure. He then decided to send me to the school nurse. I managed to persuade her that I had genuinely hurt my eye. She put an eye-patch on me and sent me back to my class. At playtime, I was able to tell all my mates what had happened. I don't think I told any of them that the accident was fake. Still, I felt so proud of myself. I had got my own back against this nasty teacher.

After two terms at my language centre, it was decided that I was ready to go to another school. This was much nearer to where we lived. Choosing the school was also an opportunity for me to make my first big decision, all on my own. I was very pleased with my new school. It was only a few minutes' walk away from our house.

My new school had excellent facilities. I later discovered that it was seen as a deprived school as it was located in one of the poorest parts of our city. But for me it was very special. Compared to where I came from, this school had everything. We had chairs and desks. We could do physical education and games. We could do a range of subjects, from reading and writing to some practical ones like metal and wood work. It has to be said, I was much better at the former.

At the end of my first term at the school, I was given a 'Report on Studies'. This outlined the progress I had made in my various subjects. It was clear English, arithmetic and mathematics were my best subjects given I was in Set 1, the top set, for these. For all other subjects I was in Set 2. It also stated the grade I had achieved. My best was in Arithmetic. I had been able to achieve a B which meant 'Good.' This was mainly because I was better than most of my class fellows at the exercises we had to do on the new currency. The country had moved over to decimalisation and it was the school's job to teach the pupils how to work out the new coins. Whereas before it was 20 shillings to a pound, with each shilling being made of 12 pence, now it was to be a straightforward system of 100 pence to a pound. Unbeknown to my classmates and teachers, I had experienced something similar in Pakistan. There, our currency used to be the rupee which was made up of 16 annas, with each anna being worth 4 paisas. Then it had moved to 100 paisas to make a rupee. So for me, the conversion methodology was almost identical and it gave me a leg up among my fellow pupils.

I did, however, regret one thing about losing the old currency. I used to like the fact that the letter 'd' was used to describe the old pennies. I had learnt that this was from the Latin word *denarius*. It was clear that the word *dinar* which the Arabs use as their currency has the same origin.

In English, I was able to achieve a 'C' which was average. But this was "A very good achievement" according to the teacher who used to teach us immigrant pupils. She said after all English was my second language. This made me feel really good. It also indirectly affirmed that I had a 'first' language.

I had to take my report home to my parents and get their signature to show they had seen it. I would have given anything to be able to show my report to my Dad and get his 'well done.' Instead, I had to put up with getting it signed by my 'father' who had brought me into England. He just signed his name when I gave him the report. He could not read much English and had no understanding of the school system and subjects, either in England or in Pakistan, since he had been to school in neither country. Unlike some in our community who simply put a cross, he was able to print his name. After a while, I stopped showing him my school reports. Instead, I used to forge his signature.

I worked hard during my three years there. I continued to do well in mathematics and English. The latter was helped by all the reading I had begun to do. In addition, I enrolled for extra study at night school. I had to get permission from my headmaster before I was allowed to attend these classes as they were meant for adults. I think I was the first pupil from our school who was this keen on education.

It was a rocky start at my new school. It took a while to be accepted by my fellow pupils especially the white ones. On the first day at my new school, the office told me to go to my class. When I arrived in the room, the teacher was not there. As soon as I opened the classroom door, a tall white boy got out of his seat and came towards me. I was still standing. He pushed me, lifted me off my feet and pushed me against the wall and said, "We don't want any more fucking pakis here." Later, I managed to get my own back. I used to deliberately mispronounce his name to make it sound like a swear word. I would blame it on the fact English was not my first language; he didn't know any better so he bought my story. Things slowly began to get better. I am not sure whether it made me feel better or not to discover that others like the writer Hanif Kureishi had also had such abuse when they were growing up. Once he said that he had experienced such abuse on a daily basis. Fortunately, my experience was not as bad.

My interests in music and literature and my fascination with and attitudes towards people who were different from me, be they white, black or Indian, slowly began to set me apart from the rest of my family and peers, most of whom were leading restricted and typically 'Pakistani' lives.

My exposure to music began with the TV programme *Top of the Pops*. Coming from a world where there was no music, you can just imagine what I thought about the bands I saw. I recall going to school and saying something like "What sort of a name is Mud for a band? Who would buy their music with a name like that?" I realised too late that one of the girls I quite liked was upset by this comment. That was her favourite band. It took some doing to dig out of that hole!

By the end of my three years at the school, I had been accepted by many of my school mates, from across all racial and ethnic groups. Music was the main way into their lives, especially those of my white and black friends. Every time I came across a new song or pop band, I would talk to them about it. They used to laugh at me, but in a friendly way, given how naive I was about a world in which they considered themselves to be experts. I remember one particular occasion which got the whole class involved (when we should have been doing more important things!). The group 10cc had just released their song *Rubber Bullets*. I was trying to describe the group and the song. So carried away was I that I even tried to sing a few of the song's lines. But this was to be my only public performance—ever!

By the time I left school, quite a few of the white pupils were treating me as a friend, even the ones who didn't like Pakistanis generally. They used to say to me, "We hate Pakis but you are alright."

This school for me was the first opportunity to get close to black people, called *sheedi* in our slang. The culture I had come from taught me to be colour prejudiced, to believe that being dark was ugly. This prejudice began to be challenged in my mind. I began to realise that my black peers were no different from the rest of us and that being beautiful was much more than the colour of one's skin.

One or two of the *sheedi* boys even became friends. There was a lot of talk about 'black is beautiful', so being black was a bit trendy. Soon, I was to discover the music of Bob Marley and add it to my list of favourite artists. But being Asian was another thing altogether. Our community was seen as passive who were expected to put up with abuse and not fight back.

The film *Enter the Dragon* had just come out at the cinemas and Karl Douglas' *Kung fu Fighting* was high in the music charts. So a few of us decided to go and see the film. I found it quite amazing to see a Chinese man, the Bruce Lee character, actually as a hero who ends up beating all the other kung fu fighters. At a time when Asians, including the Chinese, were seen as weaklings, it was great seeing this Chinese guy coming out as a winner even in fights against the white characters.

At the school, we had two Indian pupils; all other Asians were from Pakistan, mostly Mirpuris. I found myself drawn to the Indian pupils. It was later I realised that this was because of the guilt I felt due to the poor treatment of Indians by our village people at Partition time. I used to stick up for the Sikh boy who was picked on by everyone, whites and Pakistanis. They used to go up to him, usually from behind him when he was sitting in the class, and try and knock his turban off. Whenever I could, I used to sit with him; I didn't like him being on his own. I also made friends with a Hindu boy at the school. I remember him because he was called Lal, which means red in Urdu. I remember a man in our village was called Lal Hussain. Obviously, the name was common in pre-partition India.

Every morning, all the classes would gather in the big hall of the school and sing songs. One or two teachers would talk to us. Much of it I didn't understand in the early days but later began to realise it was about right and wrong, as this part of the learning day was the school assembly. I didn't really join in the singing, maybe the occasional miming. But I did read the words. Some of them were quite interesting. I particularly remember one song we used to call the 'hammer song' because it was about a man who wanted a hammer. I knew what a hammer was as the *lohar*, the blacksmith, in our village used to have one to beat his red hot metal into shape. The song had a happy ending because the man got what he wanted. It used to make me wonder what I would do with such a hammer.

I also remember that during the assembly, usually towards the end, we used to be asked, or rather told, to bow our heads. Although we didn't understand the words which spoke about our father who did art in heaven, me and some of my Pakistani friends knew this was some kind of praying, so we used to refuse to bow our heads in defiance.

I went to a local barber, a Pakistani man with a beard. He was very gentle and reminded me of my own father, probably the first man to do so. While cutting my hair, he used to give me advice on such things as writing to my parents, not going to clubs, remembering to pray and so on. Eventually, I got fed up with him and I found myself another barber nearby. He also was a Pakistani, but he didn't say much, which suited me. However, our relationship came to a head when, one day we did not see eye to eye about whether women should have their hair cut. I couldn't see anything wrong with it, saying "I think some of them look quite nice after they have been to the hairdresser." He went ballistic. "How can you be so *angraize*, white? They can do what they like but our religion teaches us it is a sin." I never did find any religious reference for this theology.

On my way to the barber's one day, I took a slight detour so I could explore more of the world around our neighbourhood. I came across the library. At the Language Centre we had been told what a library was and had been taken to the one nearby. Like the world I had left behind in Pakistan, the house we lived in had no books.

I went inside the library and, after a few minutes of looking around, I plucked up the courage to go up to the desk marked 'Reception.' There was a lady sitting behind it. I explained to her, "I was just passing by and thought I would pop in". "Would you like to join?" she said. "Join?" I said. "Yes, to become a member so you can borrow books and read them at home".

The lady gave me a form to fill in. I had to write my name and address on it. She explained that I needed to get a signature from an adult "and then you will be able to borrow books." A few days later, I took my form back, duly signed. It was explained that I could borrow up to eight books at a time and keep them for up to four weeks. She showed me the different sections of the library. I used to go there regularly. The staff who worked there got to know me very well. They knew the kind of books I liked.

During my time at school, I discovered and fell in love with English literature, beginning with Steinbeck's *The Grapes of Wrath*. This was all very unusual for a young person from my background. I waited till my next payday from my job as a paper-boy to buy my own copy of the book, at a price of 45 pence. I had the book covered in Fablon. I was advised that this adhesive clear plastic film would not only reinforce the book cover, it would protect it from damage and help to keep it clean. As my first and precious book, I certainly wanted to look after it.

People in the family I was living with could not understand why I needed to spend my own money on a book. All they could see was that I had spent nearly ten shillings which would have given me nearly 10 rupees if I had sent it to Pakistan. It might have given me even more if I had sent it through the black market methods. They thought such things as *fazool kharchi*, wastefulness. If only they knew then how much I would come to spend on books later on in life!

The book told the story of a dispossessed community driven from its land in Oklahoma as a result of industrial 'progress.' The corporations that owned the land concluded that it was more effective to replace the tenant farmers with tractors. This book had a great impact on me at an impressionable stage in my life. The story for me represented the experience of my community who had been displaced as a result of the building of the Mangla Dam. Some 100,000 people had been affected. They were promised, in return, compensation and other benefits. But would the promises be delivered?

When I read about bulldozers demolishing the tenant farmers' smallholdings and cabins, I imagined the same happening in Mirpur. There was a stubborn character, appropriately named Muley, who refused to leave his house. I imagined that there were people in Mirpur who were equally stubborn in refusing to leave their land and the graves of their loved ones. And, just as Steinbeck's displaced people were abused by their fellow countrymen—they were called *Oakies*—I heard stories of Mirpuri migrants being abused by their own countrymen and called *MPs*.

There were other aspects of The Grapes of Wrath which impacted me. Just as the Tom Joad character in the book wanted to stand up for his people and fight for justice so I imagined myself doing so too:

Like Tom Joad, I also imagined being where the hungry people were struggling to eat and defending some guy against a cop. And I imagined being there to defend people's rights to eat the food they had produced or to help them live in the house they had built.

The second book from the same time which made an impact on me was Harper Lee's *To Kill a Mockingbird*. It taught me about justice and racism. It was also significant that the white lawyer character was fighting for the rights of a black man. I thought maybe white people would do the same for me and others from my minority community. This one only cost me 35 pence. I also had it covered in Fablon. This time I decided to keep it quiet from my family. I could just hear their response: *why do you need two books? All these years, we have managed to succeed without wasting our money on such luxuries.*

These two books, which I read within a couple of years of arriving in England, are the earliest factors contributing to my understanding of people's commonalities. The fact that both of them were set in America and were about white people did not matter. They were equally relevant to me and my community. I imagined that the mother in Steinbeck's book and the father in Lee's book were mine; I wanted them to be mine.

At school I was given a prize for a special essay. It was a book. I put it on the window sill in my bedroom. Soon, I bought other books from a second hand stall near where we lived. Since then, I have acquired many other books. Too many? Surely, it's not possible to have too many books!

I wasn't given any money by the family I was living with but had an uncle who used to give me one pound whenever he came to see me, which was every month or so. To supplement this, I found myself a job with a local newsagent. I delivered newspapers to people's houses, before and after school. Some of the people I delivered to lived in big tower blocks. Although they had an electric lift to go up and down, when this did not work, I had to climb the stairs. Sometimes this could be many floors, but I didn't mind as I was used to walking. It reminded me of my long walks to school back home. Sometimes walking was preferable because the lift had been used as a toilet. Sundays were a particular challenge. The bag was very heavy as most of the newspapers had more pages. Some also had magazines with them. At the end of the week, I collected the money from the customers and took it back to the shop. I was then paid my weekly wages.

After a little while, we moved to a different house so I looked for a paper round near our new house. Although I didn't find one, there was an Indian shop which asked me if I would help distribute an Urdu newspaper, *Milaap*, to all the Pakistani houses in the area. It was free but they were hoping that after a while people would pay for it. I would be given one pence for each paper I delivered. Occasionally, I would get abuse from the Pakistanis. On one occasion a man came out of his house and shouted at me, "Here, take this and shove it up your backside!" Responses like this, plus the fact no one was willing to subscribe to it, led the whole venture to collapse. Mind you, before we reached this point, there were a few occasions when I left some of the papers in our back garden while pretending I had delivered them, in order to collect my one pence per paper.

Around this time, I also did the Pools. Once a week I visited a number of people, all white and mainly men, and collect some sort of form they had completed to win money. I am told it was a bit of gambling on football results. The key for me was that for each one I collected I was able to earn a few pence. Another method of 'making' money involved collecting Co-operative stamps from the milkman who delivered our daily milk. Each week, when he was paid, he would give us stamps, which I collected and stuck in a book he gave us. I loved licking the stamps before putting them in the book. Each complete book was worth one pound. I soon discovered another kind of stamp, the *Green Shield* stamps. To get these we had to shop at the Tesco supermarket. There was a store about a mile from where we lived. So I used to go down there with a list of things to buy just so I could get the stamps. When the book was full, instead of money, you could exchange it for gifts. To do that you had to go to their big shop in the city centre.

After a couple of years in the UK, I managed to save up enough money to buy a used tape recorder from a second-hand shop. The shop also had many other items on sale. Now I could now listen to my own choice of music at any time. I no longer had to wait for my favourite radio or TV programme. One day I decided to go to the local branch of WH Smiths. Like any newcomer to a country, I went to the counter and asked the white man sitting there to recommend some English music. He looked a bit unsure, as if I had made a strange request. He muttered something and pointed me to the wall on his left where the cassettes were. I had no idea what I was looking for. This section of the store was to become my first port of call every time I had some spare cash. Later, I discovered many other music outlets. They were called record shops and you could also pick up news of forthcoming concerts there.

I looked at the tapes. They were arranged alphabetically. One caught my eye because it had the picture of a man on the cover. I assumed this must be the singer. I bought it. It was Perry Como. I then decided to buy something which looked really quite strange. The cover did not have a picture of a human being. Instead it had a triangle with light shining through it. I later discovered it was a prism. What I thought was the singer had a funny sounding name. Why would a man be called Pink? The album was *Dark Side of the Moon*. I did not like Perry Como very much, but liked Pink Floyd and bought a few more Pink Floyd tapes. Next time I had some money, I bought the cassette *Crime of the Century* by a man named Supertramp, again by looking at the cover. It had lots of stars on it and two hands under a metal grille as if they were trying to break out of prison. My mates at school pointed out that both Pink Floyd and Supertramp were not men but names of bands. Soon after, I discovered the record *Rumours* by the band Fleetwood Mac. I especially liked one of the songs *Go Your Own Way*, even though I didn't need any such encouragement. I used to listen to it again and again and lose myself doing so.

Slowly, music came to define me. Now my *fazool kharchi*, wastefulness, was not just restricted to books. But, like literature, music would enable me to cross borders and travel into previously unknown worlds and peoples. Music became a sort of comfort blanket for me, bearing in mind the number of times I would fall asleep listening to *Echoes* or *One of these nights*.

What a wonderful country I had come to! Music became an essential part of my identity. I could not imagine an existence without it. If ever I have an opportunity to spend some quality time with myself, it is by being surrounded by all my records, having a favourite one on the turntable while I sit there exploring its cover, reading along the sleeve notes. Maybe a glass of wine, preferably red, would just complete it all. Heaven, here on earth! I wonder whether there would be music in heaven! What a silly question; how could it be heaven without it?

Going to concerts, popping into record stores, buying music papers—Melody Maker and New Musical Express were my favourites—talking to friends about what I was listening to and getting their ideas about bands I had not come across yet, it all came to be not just a part of my life; at times it was my life. Occasionally, I would go to friends' houses to listen to their record collection and make plans about some upcoming concert.

Once, a few of us drove to a nearby town to see a band called *Loving Awareness.* They were linked to the pirate radio station, Radio Caroline. Two of us spent the whole evening outside the venue because we had gone wearing *trainers,* sports shoes, and this was against their 'no trainers' rule. On another occasion, I went to a concert by the artist Steve Gibbons. It was in his back garden and had been arranged to raise money for a tombstone for one of his friends. I recall at the start of the proceedings a man stood up and read out a prayer for the dead friend. Coming from a world where music was seen as sinful, this meant a great deal to me.

Music was to become my lifelong companion. It was there at my highest and lowest moments. There were songs I would listen to when I felt sad. Once, when I was involved in a relationship which was not going to go anywhere, I found solace in the song *Lonely Man* by the singer Neil Diamond. But my all-time favourite music for these moments was *Musical Box* by Genesis. I used to put it on the turntable whenever I felt sorry for myself and wanted to make myself cry. Often, the song was long enough for doing this but there were times when I would put it on again and again. Later, other songs would also become favourites though not necessarily for the same reason. *Because the Night* by Pattie Smith and *Me and My Woman* by Roy Harper were notable amongst them.

Peter Gabriel was the front man of the band Genesis, and it was he whose voice would connect with my deepest emotions in *Musical Box.* He created a festival called WOMAD (world of music and dance). He used to bring to the UK artists from across the world. This was how I discovered the all-time greatest Pakistani qawalli singer, Nusrat Fateh Ali Khan. Watching, on YouTube, my fellow white Brits enjoying the qawalli, *Haqq Ali Ali,* reminded me of me losing myself at all the numerous rock concerts I had attended. Who needs to understand the words?

This was how I also discovered the Senegalese artist Youssou 'Dour who sang in Wolof. I did not understand a single word of what he was saying but I knew there was more to music than the words. Gabriel also endeared himself to me by writing and performing the song *Biko* about the South African activist Steve Biko, which provided a link between my music and my politics.

I began to learn about the wider world and its numerous cultures. While still at school, I started to read quality newspapers. I recall going up to one of my teachers and asking for his advice as to which newspaper I should read. He said he was a reader of the Daily Telegraph. He explained that it had the best sports coverage. I wasn't much bothered about sports and for some reason I did not take to this particular newspaper. During this 'research and trial' phase, I bought the News of the World a few times, thinking that it might have news of Pakistan given that it was 'news of the world'. I soon realised that this was just a name. Its main focus was the UK and even that wasn't brilliant. There was very little substance in it. Once, I bought a newspaper because it looked to have something about Kashmir. But, when I got home, I realised this was about a horse, not the country; it was a horse racing newspaper.

Soon, I realised that there was more to read in the bigger papers, the broadsheets and even more on Sundays. Soon, buying a Sunday paper became a habit. I used to save up for this treat, later to become my weekly fix; the texture, the smell, the look of the newspaper. I would especially look forward to some of the sections and columns of the paper.

I settled on the Sunday Times as my regular read. I can't remember how this began but I do know what hooked me on this publication. It was their focus on the 'thalidomide' story. This was a drug, given to pregnant women, which caused birth defects in many babies. The paper's 'Insight' team of journalists used to write pages and pages each week.

During these early days in England, I also discovered a programme on television which used to be broadcast on Sundays at mid-day, called Weekend World. I used to think of it as a 'newspaper on television'. It was introduced by a man called Peter Jay. A few years later, his role was taken over by another man, Brian Walden.

Coming from the somewhat religious background I had, at first I tried to keep up with my obligations and duties. Occasionally, I would say one or two of my daily prayers and would try to get along to a mosque on Fridays. But even this wasn't helped by the fact that it was difficult to find a mosque near to where we lived. And this was quite a Pakistani area. The situation was probably worse elsewhere.

But, if truth be told, the world I had arrived in had little religion in it. It was not a part of the life of the family I was staying with. I don't recall anyone praying. I don't think there was a Quran in the house. If there was, I never saw it. The talk generally was of being Pakistanis, not Muslims. So slowly but surely, religion became a foreign language for me. However, I missed some of it.

One thing as children we used to look forward to were the Eid festivals, especially the first, little Eid, which followed immediately after fasting in the month of Ramadan. But Eid now was nothing like it. In the world of my childhood which I had left behind, there was a long period of anticipation. Everyone around us knew that Eid was coming. You could sense it in the air around you. But there was nothing like that here in my new country. The world carried on as before. There was none of the anticipation we used to experience. There were no signs in the community that Eid was coming. Even on the day, many around us didn't know that it was Eid. Mind you, most didn't even know what Eid was. A few of the English people used to refer to the occasion as 'your Christmas.'

It wasn't helped by the fact that our own community didn't make much of Eid. Quite a few of the men went to work as if it was a normal day. They didn't want to lose a day's pay over it. The situation was made worse by the lack of agreement within our community as to when Eid actually was. In Pakistan, on the evening of 29th Ramadan, everyone used to look out for the new moon. If it appeared, then everyone knew Eid had come. When it didn't, we knew it would definitely be the day after. Simple. But here in England it was a very strange situation. There was often no agreement over the festival. Some in the community said it was Eid one day while the rest thought it was on another day. It all depended on whether you followed the news from Pakistan or Saudi Arabia. Eid on two separate days became a norm. One year, soon after the East Pakistan war, we had three Eids, one after the other. We had a Pakistani Eid, an Arabic Eid and a Bangladeshi Eid, named after the new country which had resulted from East Pakistan's independence.

In those days, I had begun to write letters and articles in the Urdu press. So I wrote one entitled "Is it Eid or not." The letter was printed in the Daily Jang, which used to be published from London:

> *It has become normal in Britain for us to celebrate at least two, sometime even three, Eids. Some people fast 30 days and then celebrate it, while*

others do it after 29. Some even do it after just 28 days. This happens
because after centuries of Islam, our community has not been able to
reach an agreement when Eid is. Man has gone to the moon and our
community has not been able to reach one little agreement over this
important matter.

Each year, for a few days around Eid, people write into the Urdu press
expressing their disquiet but then things go quiet until next year when
the whole thing happens all over again.

I plead with the Muslim leadership that the time has come for them to
reach agreement over this matter. Unless we gather on one platform,
nothing is going to change. If it is obligatory for us to celebrate Eid only
after the new moon is sighted then surely we can get help from science
to find out.

I gradually found that the cultural gap in my life I felt about Eid was
being filled by Christmas. A good few months before, it was obvious that
Christmas was coming. Christmas was everywhere. Shops would begin
to advertise items which they wanted their customers to buy for the
occasion. Nearer the time, the whole physical environment would begin
to have Christmas signs and symbols. In the city centre, the whole area
would be decorated by the lights. After dark, they used to look so pretty.
I had never seen anything like it where I had come from.

Later on, I got excited by the special TV programmes which were
broadcast around this time. When the Sunday papers became part of my
life, I used to like the special editions they used to produce, looking back
at the year that had gone by. One of my cousins also told me that the
week after Christmas when it was New Year, you would get to kiss white
girls under some tree that would be there just for the occasion. Sadly,
this never worked for me. Maybe I wasn't lucky enough.

Within the first few years of arriving in England I also learnt that many
in my family and community would practice their religion for show. I
suppose it was another example of what the others would say or how
they could be impressed. In reality, they were no more religious than
the next guy, whatever his colour. While at school, I once worked in a
Pakistani shop cleaning chickens. There were times when the chickens
hadn't been killed properly for them to be halal. When I mentioned to
the shop owner that I felt this was wrong, he told me to keep quiet. It was
a case of 'what the customers don't know about won't hurt them.' When

I didn't keep quiet and tried to tell some of the customers, they didn't seem to care anyway.

I found the Pakistani area I lived in to be quite an oppressive environment. Occasionally, I would venture out to other parts of the town where there were more white people. This was okay, except sometimes I felt I was being stared at by the local people. I worked out that this had something to do with my colour, so I then avoided those areas. Instead, I would go to one or two white areas where I felt welcome. There was one particular area which I enjoyed going to. It had a village centre and lots of art and book shops. There were one or two pubs which used to have concerts in the evening.

Occasionally, I would venture out of the city centre. As well as visiting the record shops, I used to look forward to going to the Christian Centre for a drink. I noticed the people who worked there were very welcoming. They seemed to be very different from many other white people I had come across.

The 'venturing out' was to get easier in later life. Having a white woman by my side and having children helped. I think it probably helped people slot me in a different category. I was no longer just an Asian/Pakistani/brown man; I was now a boyfriend/husband and a dad. Later, I was also to become more confident in such situations.

During this period, I also used to take regular trips to a big church, called a cathedral, in a nearby town. I went there on days out with my rucksack. It was my little bit of adventure. By this time, I had heard that English people went on 'holiday' once a year and went on day trips in between. This was not something anyone in our community did. Why would you go all the way to such and such place when you had no purpose there and no relatives to visit! But for me that was exactly the reason to go there. I guess even if there were relatives there, I wouldn't have visited them. By this time, my appetite for such family rituals had all but disappeared. I would just about visit people if someone was seriously ill or had died either in England or in Pakistan.

I used to sit in the big hall of the cathedral and look at the environment around me. Outside the building there were ruins. These were bits of the old cathedral left behind from when it had been bombed in the war. The band Tangerine Band once performed there. They were one of the bands whose music I used to I listen to, so seeing the concert on TV was of particular interest to me. As if having music in a religious place wasn't radical enough, the thing which fascinated me most was that although the cathedral had been bombed by the Germans not that long ago, here was a band from that country being allowed to perform in the building. Sitting on the very seats I used to sit on during my daytrips were people watching and listening to the music. This sort of thing wouldn't happen in the world I was familiar with. India was our enemy and will always be so. I thought people in my new world obviously believed in forgiveness and reconciliation.

My arrival in the UK coincided with East Pakistan becoming Bangladesh. As you would expect, at this point I was very much on the side of Pakistan and saw the East Pakistani separatists and India as the bad guys. Why would they be leaving our country, the only country which had been founded in the name of Islam? Following the mainstream Pakistani line, I used to think it was as a result of an Indian plan to take over our country bit by bit. After all, why would people object to being ruled by Mr Bhutto; hadn't he won the election? And yet at a human level, my position began to change. A couple of years later, I remember some English musicians made a film *Concert for Bangladesh* to raise funds in response to the floods in that country. I went to see the film. I remember it because at the start of the concert the Indian sitar player, Ravi Shankar, was applauded which made him laugh. He hadn't actually begun playing and was just tuning up his instrument. At the same cinema, I also went to see a film called *Gimme Shelter* by the Rolling Stones.

Around this time, there was a new radio station I discovered in the area where I lived. This went by the name of BRMB. I particularly enjoyed listening to the Rock Show in the evenings which was hosted by a man named Robin Valk. In those early days, he educated me more than most about good music. What I didn't learn from him I picked up from the *Old Grey Whistle Test*. What a weird name for a TV programme! I used to love the cartoons it used to illustrate the songs. The programme introduced me to the Eagles, who had just released *One of these nights*, as well as to many other artists.

Soon after, I discovered Bruce Springsteen through a friend. Now I was into a different kind of story. Later, I would see him face to face at concerts. His songs often made me think as if he was writing about me and my experience. The first album of his I bought was called *Born to Run*. It was memorable for many reasons but especially for its cover. This showed Springsteen and Clarence Clemons, his saxophone-playing band member, leaning against each other in a manner that demonstrated a level of intimacy which can only exist between real friends. The world I had grown up in would be comfortable with such demonstration of affection between two guys. However, what made this special was their race. Springsteen, a white guy, and Clemons, a black guy, were behaving as if they were blood brothers. The significance of the album cover can only be understood with the 1970s as a backdrop.

America had barely begun to deal with its racist past with slavery and, more recently, the Ku Klux Klan racists were very much a part of its narrative. In Britain, we were yet to enact the Race Relations Act of 1976. This would make it illegal to deny people employment and services because of their colour and would prohibit the display of signs such as 'No blacks, No Irish, No dogs.' I am not sure if there were signs saying 'No pakis.' There could have been; there was certainly the cultural backdrop for it. As children, in Pakistan, we use to hear about white people going paki-bashing. In the town where I lived, the racist party, the National Front was very active. It seems like yesterday when, while escaping the oppressive nature of my own Pakistani community, I used to find myself in areas just outside the Inner Ring road. The stares of the local white people made it clear I was on the wrong side of the tracks, in a 'no-go' area. It was around this time that I began to buy the local Evening Paper on the day after the council elections. This was so that I could monitor where National Front supporters lived. I thought it wise to avoid these areas. The same was also true in relation to certain pubs, where they served alcohol, and other large gatherings of white people. We knew that after a few drinks at a pub or with the high emotions of a football game, or both combined, white people, especially men, could be quite nasty towards our community. So, Springsteen and Clemons demonstrating such friendship meant a great deal to me and other minority people.

The only Asian music I had exposure to was through Asian films. In those days, going to the cinema was one of the main pastimes popular in our community, especially amongst younger people and those of us who were keen to push the boundaries a little, given the activity was seen as a bit risqué. I remember going to see films such as *Pakeezah, Sholay, Baharo Phool Barsao, Johny Mera Naam* and *Tehzeeb*. I especially recall seeing the Pakistani film *Dosti*. I think it was about a Kashmiri man who had gone off to England, leaving behind the girl he was supposed to marry. The way he was seen coping with the West made him seem like a simpleton. For example, he thought some manikins in a shop window were real women. Some of this portrayal offended our community. They wanted the film to be banned. But it continued to play to full houses especially after the additional publicity that resulted from the controversy.

Having heard some of these names while I was still in Pakistan, I was now able to hear the music of people such as Mehdi Hassan, Noor Jahan, Mala, Rafi and Lata Mangeshkar. I particularly liked the fact that Lata had once remarked that she had found *Bhagwan*, God, in Mehdi Hasan's voice. Maybe one day our two countries will become friends again with the help of our artistic community. I also liked the actors and actresses especially though not exclusively those from Pakistan, such as Rani, Nadeem, Shabnum, Ejaz and Waheed Murad.

All the films had lots of songs in them, which I later realised were being mimed. A few people used to take their cassette recorders to the cinema so they could record the music. When I had my own cassette machine, I decided not to take it to the cinema. However, I did try to record music from the TV programme *Nai Zindagi Naya Jeevan*, New Life, which was on the BBC on Sunday mornings. As well as music, the programme had news of Pakistan and Pakistanis in England. It was presented by Mahendra Kaul and Saleem Shahed.

I used to put the cassette machine right next to the TV. Although it did record, the quality was never very good. Soon I was to discovered that you could buy music cassettes from the shops. There was a Pakistani company called the Oriental Star Agencies which used to produce these. My favourite was one by Shokat Ali which had songs like *Jab Bahar Aai To Sehra Ki Taraf* I also liked his song *Challa*, as this told the story of an Asian immigrant and his experiences in England. I liked him especially because of his singing of Saif ul Malook, a kind of very long poem which had been written by Mian Muhammad Bakhsh, a Sufi saint who came from near Azad Kashmir and who wrote in Punjabi/Pahari. Even in our non-musical world, as a child, I had heard of Saif ul Malook from my elders. The emphasis in the singing/recitation is purely on the human voice. I especially like the beginning of the poem which goes *Dushman maray tey khushi na kariay*, don't rejoice when your enemy dies, (because one day it will be you).

I later discovered that Oriental Star Agencies had worked with Peter Gabriel in bringing Nusrat Fateh Ali Khan to the attention of the western audiences. Around this time I briefly encountered the music of Pathana

Khan. I loved its simplicity; it had a certain purity about it. On one or two occasions, I went to *mushairas*, Urdu poetry readings, but the activity lost out to my concerts

I liked the fact that in the world of films, music and art, there was little distinction between Indians and Pakistanis. They happily came together to appreciate them. Perhaps, one day, it will be like this elsewhere.

I had never been a sporting kind. Other than joining in with a bit of volleyball or kabaddi, I spent most of time with 'clean' and safe activities where there was no chance of getting dirty or hurt. This continued in England. I did, however, try to become involved in football. This was mainly restricted to watching Match of the Day. I did go to a football match once but found the atmosphere very aggressive and threatening. I had gone with some white friends. I wondered whether if I had gone on my own or with other Pakistani friends I might have been abused by racists.

Once, I went to watch a kabaddi match. This was held at the local stadium and was between a Pakistani team and a team of players from the local Sikh Temple. The organisers kept stressing that this was a friendly competition. I think they did not want it become some nationalistic event between the two countries. They managed to achieve their aims. Not only were teams from our two communities playing on the field, both communities were present amongst the few thousand spectators. The local Member of Parliament presented the trophy and the medals to the players. He commented that there should be more such events which would bring the diverse communities together. He said sport was probably the best vehicle for doing this. The event was well covered in the Pakistani newspapers, although I thought it was a bit ambitious to liken it to the FA Cup, which was how the Daily Jang, the London Urdu newspaper, put it:

> At least 5000 people turned up at a local stadium to watch a traditional Indian sport called Kabaddi. Now arrangements are going ahead for the next big game—described as 'like rugby but without the ball'. The organiser was quoted as saying "we think it could eventually rival football. The game is tremendously popular in India and Pakistan and it could catch on here—perhaps even being taught in schools.

Through the TV programmes and Asian newspapers, I began to develop a wider awareness of my community and its needs. Once I wrote to the UK Islamic Mission in London offering to work for the good of my community. I had a reply from their Secretary General:

Dear Brother in Islam

Assalamo Alaikum

Thank you for your offer to do some volunteer social work in the local hospitals and prisons. Your name and address has been noted down for future reference. We are trying to get the information of all the hospitals and the prisons where our help will be needed. We will let you know when and where your help will be needed. With kind regards and best wishes

Yours brotherly

I was conscious of being 'different' from my community. I once gave an interview to a journalist in which I said, with some pride, that I was an oddity. Little did I know! I was being prepared to go against the grain even more later on.

During this period, I also began to gain further understanding of the poor treatment of women in our community. The family I was staying with had quite a few daughters. I recall every time a new child was born, I could tell its sex by simply looking at the father's face when he returned from the hospital. If it was a girl, he would look as if someone had died. And yet, when they and others in our community had a boy, they would congratulate each other and distribute sweets in the community.

I left school at sixteen because I needed to support myself. I had been fortunate to be as old as that, as far as my passport went anyway. Around that time the age at which one could leave school had been changed from 15 years to 16. This explains why from time to time a group of us pupils were referred to as *rosla* kids, in reference to the 'Raising of the School Leaving Age.' Had this not happened, goodness knows what would have happened to me. At that critical stage in my life, an extra year of school made all the difference in helping me to adapt to my new country. It also helped me to achieve a few qualifications which got me started on the qualifications ladder. I didn't know then that, one day, this would lead to two university degrees and much more besides.

In my end-of-school examinations, I had managed to achieve 4 out of 5 of the CSEs, certificate of secondary education. The best result was in Mathematics where I had achieved a grade 1. This meant that it was equivalent to an Ordinary Level, which would later help me to get into school teaching. In English, I had been able to achieve a grade 3. I was pleased with it. I knew I would be able to improve on it in later life. My School Leaving Certificate acknowledged my achievement in this respect. It stated:

> *K is a very smartly dressed boy who cares about his appearance. He has made great efforts to improve his standards of English by a good deal of reading encouraged by many members of staff. This initiative applied to language improvement has also stood him in good stead with his prefect duties where he has been friendly but firm as required and proved a most capable interpreter.*

> *In our social games he has a decided liking for Lawn Tennis at which he has become quite proficient.* (I had pretensions to be Ilie Nastase, who was the best player around at this time and looked a bit Pakistani)

I then looked for work. The first job I found, with the help of my school, offered me £10 a week wage. I was told that at the end of the year this would go up to £11 and then a year later to £12. Then someone told me about a Careers Officer. Without telling my school, I went to see him. This paid off. With his help I managed to obtain a clerical job at a local factory. This paid quite a few more pounds each week. But I benefited much more than just money from this job.

This was a training job in administration. During the first two years, I had an opportunity to work in a number of different departments, learning whatever it was they did by being shown the ropes by various people in the department. At the end of the training, I was told there was a permanent job in one of the departments. Once a week, I was sent to college to continue my education. I was paid my wages even for that day I was at college—it was called a salary since I was a white collar worker. The employer also paid my course fees. This pleased my parents no end, especially my father. He felt guilty for sending me, his only son, to England and thus interrupting my education in Pakistan. He knew here in England I had no choice but to leave school and go to work. But, now it was all okay. I was going to continue my education while earning a living in an office-based job, not in a dirty factory where most of our community worked.

It goes without saying that college study would prove beneficial for me and build on the foundations already laid through my education both in Pakistan and England. But I was to achieve much more during the remaining four days of my week.

We had a training officer to oversee our training. He was quite a wise man who generously imparted to us much that was valuable. On the first day, he told us it was important to dress appropriately. For example, if we were working on the factory floor, we should come to work in our jeans and if we were office-based then it should be a suit, or at least a jacket and trousers, with a tie. He also said it was very important to make friends with the support staff; the lady who brings the tea, the man who brings the post and the switchboard ladies.

This was also when I gained for myself a 'nick name.' On our first day, we were all asked to introduce ourselves. When it was the turn of us Pakistanis, the training office said, "Have you got like a nickname which would be easier for us to pronounce?" I came up with Ken; well, it was as close to my name as I could get and, as an English name, I knew it would be easier for my workmates. The other Pakistani also came up with one. I am not sure whether, like me, he had just made it up. I guess this was a reminder that we were in a foreign country and we had to fit in on the terms dictated by the majority, even if it meant changing our beautiful names to something a little easier for our English neighbours.

The employer I worked for was one of the nationalised, government-owned, industries. I quickly realised that within the workforce there was a hierarchy. At the bottom were the factory floor workers. These were mainly Pakistani and black immigrants and a few white men who seemed not to have done well at school. I met a few of their ilk at the school I attended. I used to think they had a very poor attitude towards education and little respect for teachers. Although I was an immigrant who had to learn English from scratch, I was conscious that at times I was doing better than them.

Unlike us, the factory workers were paid weekly wages. The toilets they used did not have toilet paper so the workers had to bring their own from home. Mind you, they did not help their case. At times they would steal the light bulbs from the toilets . . . They had to pay a 10 pence deposit for their cutlery in their own separate canteen. After finishing their meal, they would take their dirty knife and fork back in order to get the money back. Those of us who were office staff had a much better eating space. We did not have to pay a deposit for our cutlery. I used to hear about another dining facility which was exclusively set aside for the really senior staff in the company.

The canteen ladies, who I had made friends with, looked after me well. I explained to them that I did not eat meat that was not *halal.* They would provide a vegetarian option for me. For three days, I would be given cheese salad and on Friday I would be given pilchards instead of the cheese.

Coming to this workplace as a sixteen year old was a God-send for me. It gave me an opportunity to meet a wide range of people. I made friends with white people and black people, men and women. I also had a Sikh friend. Occasionally, we would go out for a drink or a bite to eat at lunch for a change from the canteen food.

During my time in this country I began to develop an awareness of community needs. On one occasion, I organised a football match to raise money for a local charity. I also organised a cultural evening so the white people could learn about Asian culture, music and food. Little did I know then that a few years later I would be organising training programmes in order to help raise awareness amongst white professionals of multi-racial society, especially of the Asian community.

After a few years of working in this job, I bought my own house. It was joined on to houses on both sides. It was possible for next door neighbours to hear each other. Perhaps one day I will live in a house which is not joined on one side; a semi-detached house. Who knows, one day I might even live in one which is completely separate from the neighbours' houses; a detached one. I knew some white people lived in such houses, but no one in our Pakistani community did. For the time being this house was my everything, my prized possession. I was a proud owner of a property that had been bought with my own hard-earned cash.

The house had two bedrooms and a bathroom upstairs and two living rooms downstairs, known as the front room and the back room and a kitchen. There was a little garden in the front which separated the house from the pavement and the road. At the back, there was a bigger garden where I began to grow vegetables like coriander and garlic so I could remember my Mum's little vegetable patch back in our village.

Buying a house was an odd thing to do for someone at my age, still in his teens. Even when doing so, normally one would turn to one's family to raise the money. This would be through the *kameti* system. This was a bit like the old English Friendly Society system. Members would pay a set amount each week and then draw from it as their turn came or when the need arose. But, given my determination to do my own thing, I raised the £500 deposit completely on my own. I opened an account at a local building society and put money in the account whenever I could. It took me about a year to save up the amount I needed.

The building society gave me a mortgage. This was a loan of £4500. It is possible that I was the first one in our *biraderi*, extended family, to get a mortgage. Although it would take me quite a few years to pay back the loan, at least I had managed to buy my house all on my own effort, without any help from my relatives. Many of them couldn't understand how I had done it. Mind you, by this time, many of them couldn't understand me, period!

Now I had even more freedom. Well, you can imagine: early adulthood, own income, own house, parents far way . . . I did what I felt like. If it was against some rule somewhere (social, religious), then the key was whether I could get away with it.

There is a practice in our community called *lena-dena*, taking, giving. It's done at various occasions such as birth of a son or wedding. It's generally the responsibility of women to keep an eye on who gave your family what amount of money on what occasion so that you could pay it back next time they have a similar occasion. It was important to pay back a little more than you had received; to give the same amount would be seen as an insult as if you were returning their gift. To give less would, I guess, mean you were exploiting the relationship. Initially, I took part in the practice at weddings by giving money, called *nindra*. However, gradually I stopped going to these gatherings, unless it was a close relative whose son or daughter was getting married. The nindra is also given in the hope that one day you will get married and you will get the money back. Since, I had no intention of wanting a family wedding, I saw it as money down the drain.

Living on my own was lonely at times. I kept myself busy with attendance at evening classes. Other than the occasional social activity, studying in the evenings became my social life. My aim was to achieve five Ordinary and two Advanced level qualifications so that I could go to university.

It was also quite hard to live on my own. Ours is a culture where men did not cook when women were around. This meant I had no idea about cooking. Throughout the years at my school in England, I was not taught any domestic skills. There was a subject called 'home economics' but it was not available for us boys; presumably, they thought we would have wives to look after us. We boys instead took subjects like woodwork and metalwork which proved to be absolutely useless for me.

Slowly, I managed to learn the basics. Initially, I relied on packet and tin food. I had some favourites. I used to love *Smash*. This was mash potatoes in a packet. All I had to do was pour boiling water on it. Another favourite was *Homepride* curry cook-in-sauce. It was quite sweet, English style curry, not the Asian style.

Because I had little money after paying my mortgage and other household expenses, it was difficult to afford food at times. Some days, I recall I just had 20 pence. So I would buy a potato and make chips which I had with a fried egg. On some occasions, I would have milky tea with sugar about an hour before lunch and then I would go to sleep. This meant I was able to miss lunch. Then, I would make myself go on until the evening without eating.

Occasionally, I would visit relatives around meal times. When I thought they were going to be eating soon, I would get up to go. They would then ask me to stay for the meal. Of course, I couldn't accept straight away, otherwise they would think I was desperate (I was, but that's beside the point). I would refuse a couple of times and then accept their offer. I had to go through the motions in this situation but not refuse food too seriously.

On very rare occasions, I was able to save up and treat myself at the local Pakistani cafe-restaurant. My favourite was called Shereen Kadah. These were days, long before the development of the Balti restaurants, when such eateries did not have printed menus. I would arrive and, just like I had seen people do in Pakistan, I would ask what they had cooked.

My favourite was chicken curry with spinach which I would have with tandoori roti to remind me of my mother's cooking.

Around this time, I was conscious that I should be settling down with a wife. One or two older Pakistani friends tried to arrange a marriage for me. I remember going to a family's house with one of these friends. After a little while, a young girl came in with a tray of drinks. She said nothing, nor did anyone else. I remember she put the tray down and went out. I thought this to be very strange. According to my way of seeing things, I should at least get to know the girl, we should go out a few times, discuss our ideas and expectations. Of course, this British way of doing things was alien to the Pakistani community. So this was yet another confirmation that we had different ideas about life . . .

Once, I came across a TV programme, *Here Today Here Tomorrow*. It was made by a famous Pakistani actor by the name of Zia Mohyeddin. It included interviews with Asians, young and old. I remember one in particular where a young Pakistani, about my age, was saying that he felt quite odd in his community, because he was not married. He seemed quite proud of his oddity. I recall thinking how his comment summed me up exactly.

Occasionally, white friends used to say that I would meet the right girl one day and fall head over heels in love and then live happily ever after. I didn't believe them. How would I know when it happens? Friends also said that maybe if I got to university, I would meet the love of my life there. Some would joke that I would find a village girl 'back home.' This was not funny, I thought. In a strange way, it strengthened my resolve not to have my marriage arranged by my parents. At this stage in my life, I had no idea what was to come.

Around the time I moved into my own house, I had also managed to save up my plane fare to go and visit my parents. It had now been eight years since we had seen each other. A lot had happened during that time. But there were two versions of my story. One version, the sanitised version, was known by my parents and some childhood friends. The rest was only known by me and a few others close to me in England.

Whenever he had the chance to talk about me, my father would tell people that I was doing well. I had left school and was now working in a factory. No, this was not a dirty job on the factory floor but in the office. I was in a training role for two years, learning all the jobs which are normally done by *gorey*, white, officers. One day a week the government (was it the Queen herself?) was paying for me to go to college where I was learning (he would then give it added emphasis) *National Certificate in Business Studies.* I was such a good boy, unlike the others. Instead of spending my time going out to clubs and pubs, I was studying in the evenings too. "He comes home from work, eats something and then goes out to his classes. By the time he finishes the class and gets back home, it is time to go to sleep." He would explain that although I was having to pay for this myself, it was worth it. It would mean an even better job one day, with more money and more respect.

He would go onto explain that I was saving up to buy my own house. "No one has even done this in our family," he would point out, "and at such an early age as well." He would go into detail of how I had saved some of the money and borrowed the rest from the bank, not relying on favours from relatives.

But there was much more that happened during these eight or so years I had been away from my parents. I had become my own person. It was clear in my mind what my future would look like. I knew, for example, that one day I would marry a woman of my own choosing.

During this period, I aspired to be a writer. I joined a local writers group where I wrote a play which had a young Pakistani as the main character. In one of the scenes, he says to his parents that he would decide who to marry and that his wife would be someone who speaks her mind. Contrary to our culture where women were seen as property, he wanted a wife who would be a companion.

The world around me

I was slowly becoming aware of the wider society around me. To begin with, this was comprised of the Pakistani people who were not related to our family. While still at school, I began to write essays. After winning a prize for an English essay, I took part in an Urdu essay competition organised by the Academy of Urdu Studies, based in Dartford. I also wrote letters and articles for the Urdu press. At first this was for the local community newspaper but later I also wrote for the national, weekly paper.

Later, my subject matter broadened to other Asians including Indians and Bangladeshis, people who until then I saw as the enemy. Still later, I included black people and eventually the mainstream white society. My identity followed a similar journey. To begin with, I belonged to the *jats* in my village. Just as I was becoming familiar with the wider community in Mirpur, I was sent to the UK. Here, I soon became a Pakistani. The wider community around us referred to us from time to time as 'Asian,' so I became an Asian. The category referred to all the peoples from the Indian sub-continent and included Pakistanis, Indians, Bangladeshis and Sri Lankans. I then became 'black.' In those days, anyone who was not white and who moved amongst the kind of people I did, was encouraged (if not expected) to see themselves as black. Although I became comfortable, albeit slowly, with using this term about myself, there were some in our community who could not bring themselves to be seen in the same category as people much darker.

I also belonged to a range of political action and pressure groups. This included: Campaign for Nuclear Disarmament, Rock against Racism, Indian Workers Associations, Pakistani Workers Association, Kashmiri Workers Association. You name it; I was in it. I had their badges and t-shirts. Sometimes I didn't even know what the groups actually stood for. It was a fashion thing, part of my identity. In the early days, I remember someone pointed out to me that the CND badge I was wearing was upside down. On one occasion, I also got into serious trouble for calling a couple of women lesbians. I meant feminists.

A couple of years after leaving school, I recall going to a demonstration against the National Front. It was organised by an organisation called *Searchlight*. Its leader was a man by the name of Maurice Ludmer, who was a Jew. In our community, we were told that Jews were bad people because of their association with Israel and the mistreatment of Palestinians. I remember thinking this Ludmer fellow is not bad; perhaps he is an exception. At the demonstration there were banners making statements such as 'Equality Now' and 'Labour Campaign Against Racialism' and a couple that just said *Bangladeshi Workers Association* and *Indian Workers Association*. I wondered if one day there would be a Pakistani Workers Association. There were also banners saying NEVER AGAIN! Someone explained to me that this was a reference to Hitler in Germany killing many thousands of Jews and that we didn't want such an evil to be repeated here in Britain. I agreed. Events like these made me think very positively about white people who were fighting for the rights of minorities like the Pakistani community.

This was a time when it was believed that Asians were a passive bunch. We were seen as people who did not fight back. This was all to change thanks to a group of Asian, mainly Pakistani, guys. They came to be known as the 'Bradford 12' after the town they came from. They were caught making petrol bombs but were let off on grounds of self-defence. Their lawyer, Gareth Peirce, who in my naivety I thought was a man, convinced the judge that these young men had no other option but to defend their community from the racist threat.

I also remember the Grunwick dispute. This challenged the stereotype of Asian women as passive, stay-at-home beings. You could not ask for a better example. Jayaben Desai, was the leader of the strikers. I used a picture of her as a wall-poster, which I had cut out of the newspaper, Morning Star. The image of her clad in a sari, clutching her handbag, and standing up to the powerful group of police said it all. Everyone in our community talked about this dispute that involved all these Indian women in conflict with their boss who was a brown *gora*, white man. The women in our extended household were fascinated by the fact that these Indian women were leading the strike. "And here are we who can't even go out without our men!" they used to say. Another point of conversation was centred on the fact that the strike had the support of many white workers across the country. Apparently, in the past there had been similar strikes by black and Asian workers which had not been supported by the whites.

Rock Against Racism provided a similar backdrop for my political education. This was a banner under which concerts and music events were organised to protest against racism. It had come about because of some drunken comments by Eric Clapton in support of the racist National Front. He said something like, "Blacks should be sent back to where they came from." I liked Clapton; I had his poster on my wall. In most Pakistani households, hanging on walls are usually posters depicting the names of Allah and the Prophet Mohammed (peace be upon him) or a photograph of the Kaaba in Mecca. I guess at this time, Clapton for me was more meaningful than any religious symbol. Incidentally, his fans used to scrawl graffiti on walls stating "Clapton is God." While I did not go this far, I struggled to cope with his comments. I used to make excuses for him on the basis that he was drunk. I couldn't come to terms with the fact that someone whose music I liked was actually supporting the racists who, if they came to power, would send people like me out of the country.

I used to look forward to the RAR events. They were always multi-cultural gatherings, mainly black and white people. The few Asians who came were more likely to be Indians from East Africa, who had been kicked out of Uganda and Kenya during their 'Africanisation' movements. I used to feel really comfortable at these gatherings. Mind you, it wasn't that I ever had any problems at any of the other concerts I went to, but I thought to myself that the RAR events would definitely not attract anyone who was a racist.

I also felt something special towards the many musicians who played at these events because of their commitment to eradicate racism in England and South Africa. In relation to the latter, I was quite active in the Anti-Apartheid Movement whose aim was to bring about racial justice in that country. In the early days, I didn't fully understand what the fuss was about. It just meant wearing the t-shirt and the badge but later I learnt the details of all the injustice in that country and the denial of equal opportunities for the majority black population. During this period in my life, I learnt the salutary lesson that even in fair countries such as Britain, rules are bent to suit the favoured.

There was a young white South African woman called Zola Budd who was a runner. She wanted to take part in the Olympics but could not because of the sport boycott of South Africa. An English newspaper, usually quite racist and rightwing, decided to support her case and wanted her to be given British nationality so that she could take part in the international sporting competition by representing Britain. Apparently, her father or a grandfather had British connections. For me, it boiled down to the fact she was white; nothing else. I think it took the government ten days to decide on her application. Normally, for Asians and other minorities, such processes can take many years and even then the application can be refused.

Anyway, Budd was now British but had to become a member of a British sports club before she could compete in the Olympics. Again, no problem. A club in the south of England obliged. I wondered whether they allowed membership to black and Asian people who actually lived in the country!

It was quite amusing, although sad for this fragile looking 17 year old, long way from home, that she came seventh, or something low, in her race. I recall there was a controversial collision between Budd and another runner. Although, British nationality is usually only given to people who are committed to living in the country, Budd clearly had no such intention and returned to her parents in South Africa soon after the competition. It was a useful reminder that my new country was not perfect after all, especially if you had the wrong skin colour.

I particularly appreciated the ethnic diversity in my new country and I took whatever opportunities I could to promote intercultural understanding. Generally this could involve my countrymen and a range of other communities, white or black. But my particular focus was on the Bangladeshi and Indian communities. As well as personally learning about them, I aimed to build bridges between them and my own Pakistani community. I began to belong to new groups which were set up to promote community relations amongst our community as well as with reference to other communities. A number of these groups drew their membership from across the Asian communities. It really gave me a kick to be associating with Indians and Bangladeshis who were seen by many in the Pakistani community as the enemy. I, on the other hand, saw the world differently. We were all in a foreign country together. We needed to put our past behind us and live peaceably with each other.

One of the groups I belonged to, *Asian Youth and Community Organisation,* tried to organise cultural evenings which emphasised this idea. Our programme included a social evening in my factory where white people could come and experience Asian culture. Later, as a part of our attempt to raise political awareness amongst our young people and stress our common Asian heritage and struggle, we were to organise a play about the 1919 events in Jalian Wallah Bagh where the British General Daya shot many helpless people at a demonstration.

Once, I even went to a Sikh temple. The significance of this little act can only be appreciated in the context of the conflict-based history of Indian and Pakistani peoples. The visit came about through one of the Sikh pupils at the school where I worked as an interpreter.

We sat in a big hall and listened to some religious chanting. I managed to pick up the occasional word because although it was in Indian Punjabi, some of the words were the same as in Pakistani Punjabi, which is quite close in vocabulary to our language. The Sikh holy book, the *Guru Granth Sahib,* was on a stand at the front of the hall. Sitting next to it was a man who looked holy.

During a break in the proceedings, while I was having a drink, one of the Sikh elders started to lecture me on the importance of wearing a turban. I then realised that I had blended so well into the Sikh crowd that he thought I was a Sikh youth who had turned away from his religious practices. When I pointed out that I was a Pakistani he asked whether I was a Sikh or *Musselman,* Muslim. At first I thought this was a strange question; why would a Pakistani be anything other than a Muslim? Later in our conversation, he pointed out that there was a city in Pakistani Punjab, near Lahore, which is called Nankana Sahib. It is named after the first Guru of the Sikhs, Guru Nanak Dev, who was born there. I discovered that the city is a popular pilgrimage site for Sikhs from across the world. Recognising that I was an outsider who was visiting their temple and learning about their religion, he gave me a guided tour. I especially liked the *langar,* Punjabi for free food, served in a Gurdwara. He explained that they only served vegetarian food so to ensure that all people, regardless of their dietary restrictions, can eat as equals. He said the langar was open to Sikhs and non-Sikhs alike so I would be welcome to come anytime. It's a shame that, when I was living on my own, there was not a *langar* nearby. Otherwise this would have been a great way of getting some free food.

Having begun to realise what many communities were doing and achieving in our country, I came to the conclusion that the Pakistani community needed to change. I felt they needed to learn from the success of others around them. By always looking back to where they had come from, I felt they were missing out on all the opportunities their new country had to offer. They needed to make their new country their home.

I was making England my home and I expected, or rather hoped, that my community would do the same. By this time, I had discovered the Urdu press. My favourite was the weekly newspaper *Mashriq*, which was the first Urdu newspaper started by a man named Mahmood Hashmi. For his achievement, he was referred to as *baba-e-Urdu*, father of Urdu. I also read another weekly the *Akhbar-e-Watan*. Within a couple of years of leaving school, I began to write letters and articles for some of these Urdu papers. These included the following:

- **Teaching of Urdu in English schools**: the potential role for Urdu speakers who also had teaching skills. In addition, I felt the community needed to produce teaching and learning materials which would make the best use of modern methods of education, for example flash cards and picture books instead of importing out-dated Urdu primers from Pakistan. I also said that I wished to start a campaign to keep Urdu alive and invited others to join me.

- **We don't need Pakistani political parties in England**: I felt that people who wished to establish such parties did no favours to their community but instead were giving us a bad name. If such people wish to do some good, then they should become active in the politics of this country. "We are here. This country is ours; it is our home now. We should help build our home so that it prospers. There are plenty of problems which our community faces here. What good will Pakistani political parties do in response to the National Front and individuals such as Enoch Powell and Kingsley Read?" I went onto advise our leaders to encourage our community to learn the ways of this country and become integrated into society here, working with other ethnic groups, for our mutual benefit.

- **The wider needs of the Pakistani community**: I attempted to make the case that we should adopt the good from this society and discard the bad from its own culture. I pointed out that while other communities were making progress, we were actually going backwards. We should try to follow Islam without becoming extremists. I also suggested to parents that they should play an active role in their children's lives, attending parents' evenings at schools. I made a plea for greater freedom and opportunities for girls to participate in education and recommended that parents should not press their young people into getting married before they were ready or against their will. "It is their life, not their parents'." I suggested that the community should provide opportunities for young people to meet others of the opposite sex so they could make an informed decision about their future partners. I made a case for religious education for Muslim young people within the school environment as well as teaching of Urdu so that they could keep in touch with their heritage. I also stressed the importance of leisure time, because "All work and no play makes Jack a dull boy."

I don't know whether anyone listened to my views. At least it made me feel better to get them off my chest!

I don't know what my parents had expected to find when they met me after eight years. Little did they realise the extent of influence on me from this other world with its sights, sounds and smells, its freedom and opportunities. It was a new world I had created around me with its own structures and systems. This had become my new security blanket to take the place of the one I had left behind. Following in the footsteps of Bruce Springsteen, I saw myself *Born to Run* with my own Wendy or travelling along *Thunder Road* or just having some fun hiding in the *Backstreets*. Many years later, I would have my own *Independence Day* when I would have my first argument with my father, just like Bruce talked about at the start of his song in the version included in the box set. Without a doubt, Springsteen would be my number one artist on my desert island. He would become the single most influential artist in my life and would go on to be the third party in my relationship with my dear wife. He even managed to make a link with another part of me when he discovered John Steinbeck and produced *The Ghost of Tom Joad* following my favourite, *The Grapes of Wrath*. Later, I would discover a British story teller by the name of Seth Lakeman and lose myself in his music (*Take no Rogues*, with Ben Nicholls on double bass, is just heavenly!)

Leaving and cleaving

Given it was a world in which there were no telephones, I did not hear my parents' voices for eight years. My main link with them was through letters. My father had only attended school for about three or four years but his Urdu was good enough to write to me. It is worth pointing out that the local language spoken in the Mirpur area of Pakistan is a dialect related to Urdu, which in Britain is known as Mirpuri or *Pahari*. But this is only spoken, not written, because it is not taught in schools. So when people need to write something they use Urdu.

The letters that people wrote were very formal. They followed a certain format. And my father's letters were no different. Their formality aside, they were special for me. I would keep each and every one somewhere safe and read them again and again, especially if ever I felt low. The letters became my comfort blanket.

The letters would start with '786', which is the numerological equivalent of *Bismillah ir-Rahman ir-Rahim,* meaning "I begin with the name of Allah, the beneficent and the merciful." Sometimes, he would write the numbers in English and at other times in Urdu, or use a stamp to print out the Arabic words. The following letter is quite typical, both in its format and content:

Dear Son,

Assalamu alaikum (peace be upon you). *We are all well and pray to God Almighty for your wellbeing.*

We received your letter. I am sorry it has taken us a long time to reply. Now, one of your friends is coming to England so we are sending a note with him.

Your mother, your sisters S and F are well. Your Nana sahib and Nani sahiba (maternal grandparents), *Mami sahiba* (maternal uncle's wife) *and her two children T Mohammed and S bibi are well. Your aunty R* (stepmother) *has not been well for about a month. She is better now. Write to her at her home.*

Send us a photograph of yourself so it can reassure us, especially your mother. She says it has been such a long time, she can't remember what you look like. Also, you say your college course is going to finish in the summer, do try to come and see us after.

As to the matter of your marriage, we all—your mother, your sisters, me—feel that it should be done according to our say so. You are our only son, after all!

I wrote to you about some possible rishtay, marriage proposals. *You can make your final decision when you come and you have had a look for yourself. We look forward to having your wedding celebration; you are after all our only son. It is all up to Allah Almighty.*

Your sister S is fine and so are her children. Your young sisters both attend school (meaning they go to someone's house for lessons in Urdu, Arabic and morality). *They both want watches so please send with someone who is coming back. Also, send kameez shalwar material for your mother. Make sure it is thick and warm as cold days of winter are fast approaching.*

Pass our greetings to your Mama (maternal uncle). *Ask him to send money to his family. As for you, if you have any spare cash, send it to us. But make sure you don't send it through the black market. This deprives the country of much needed foreign exchange. Send it through the Pakistani bank.*

Love from your stepmother. Love from your mother again. She is missing you very much. She keeps reminding me how long it has been since you left us. Sometime, she blames me for sending you away. Son, make plans to come home soon. It doesn't have to be long. Your mother says, if you haven't got airfare, she will pay it (she had no income source of her own).

Greetings from my work colleagues. G (he was at school with me) *has been promoted. He is the manager now. Write to him to congratulate him. He often talks about you. I showed him your photograph.*

That's it. Nothing else comes to mind. Please forgive us for any inappropriate words we may have written.

We all look forward to hearing from you and one day seeing you.

Khudaa-haafiz (God's protection)

Although he was many miles away from me, this did not stop my father parenting me. He tried his best and used his letters to offer me advice:

1. *Spend all your time in praise and worship of Allah*

2. *Remember your parents*

3. *Visit close family especially if someone is ill in hospital*

4. *Always attend funerals and write to family members in Pakistan where there might have been a death*

5. *Do not take bribes in your work dealings*

6. *If there is someone who needs your personal time then do your best to help him. Go with them to help sort it*

He would also enquire about the minutiae of my life: how do I feed myself, what do I eat, do I make *roti*, Pakistani flat bread, has the building work on my house finished, how do I get to work or college, do I get paid weekly or monthly. On one occasion he asked me what other Pakistanis thought about my achievements. Did they think I had done well?

In one letter he began by asking me to visit them. Then he went on to say that I should send them money so that they could marry one of my young sisters and meet the cost of her dowry. He then explained that it was my duty as a Muslim. "Allah says, when one's daughter or sister is of the age, she should be married off."

A few years after my arrival in England, it became possible to send tape recordings back home. Some in our village had cassette recorders that their relatives had brought back from England. Although such things could be purchased in the big towns and cities in Pakistan, such places were further away than England in many people's minds. Towns like Birmingham and Bradford were more familiar to them than the cities of Pakistan. In any case, to buy things in Pakistan means they don't have the 'Made in England' label which had such prestige locally, much more than 'Made in Pakistan'. After a while 'Made in Japan' also had some status. It didn't matter if you didn't have your own tape recorder. It was a world when such things were shared. They were seen as common village property.

Unlike letters, the tape-recordings had life in them. People could hear their loved one talking in their own local dialect.

Throughout my life in England I looked for mother or father figures. These were men and women who had some quality or attribute which reminded me of my parents. At school, I was seen as a model student as I responded with a very positive attitude to my teachers. Mind you, it was helped by the fact that I had brought with me, from my childhood, the instruction that teachers were our spiritual parents, who were to be respected in the same way we would respect our own parents.

Perhaps, once or twice, this search for parents got me into somewhat deep water. There was a white man who used to come to our school and give us rides in his expensive car. The Pakistani boys were fascinated with his story. He had two names; an English name and an Arabic one which he used on his trips to Tunisia. I liked him. There were things about him, his fine features and gentle character, which reminded me of my own father. One day, he invited me to his house. This was in a very posh part of the town. After a little while, he tried to get a bit too friendly with me. I told him to stop and he did. Goodness knows what I would have done if he hadn't.

There have been many other, more positive, relationships, with both men and women. At school I used to go to my friends' houses and be looked after by their mothers. This reminded me of my own mother. Later, these Pakistani mothers were joined by an English mother of a friend. Clearly, by this time, I was not fussed by the fact that she was from another race or ethnic group. These women gave me an opportunity to experience normal family life. I could imagine what life would have been like had I stayed with my own Mum or if she had come to England with me. I knew that a number of my Pakistani friends were also away from their real parents.

Although, this search for parents continued for many years, the process of 'leaving and cleaving' which took place in my life was foreign to my parents. Almost from day one of arriving in England, I began to take a different route from the rest of my community. Above all, I valued education. I saw it as my salvation. Many years later, I came across this quote from one of my heroes, Nelson Mandela, which sums up my own attitude in this respect:

> *Education is the great engine of personal development. It is through education that the daughter of a peasant can become a doctor, that the son of a mineworker can become the head of the mine, that a child of farmworkers can become the president of a great nation. It is what we make out of what we have, not what we are given, that separates one person from another.*

Whether this was due to my attitude towards education, my interest in books and music, my views about others different from me or my position on Pakistani women's rights, my views were different from those of my community. But probably one of the biggest changes that had taken place in me, as far as my parents were concerned, was to do with religion. Unlike others in my community, I had begun with quite a religious upbringing. But given that, for me, my religion and Pakistani culture was one and the same thing, when the environment around me changed, I began to breathe a different kind of air. I began to move into the mainstream British culture and its values, and I gradually stopped *practising* my religion. I slowly developed my own unique world, not an extension of, but separate from, that of my family and community. The world I moved in, which comprised mainly white people, did not practice any kind of religion. Many in that world thought religion to be 'gobbledy-gook,' and some were actually opposed to it. Here I discovered words such as atheist and agnostic. Some of my new friends were actually anti-religion.

And yet, many of my new friends were decent folk. They would do anything to help create a welcoming society so people like me could flourish. It certainly helped to provide freedom and space for me to establish myself and develop a new identity in my adopted country.

I realised that I was entering an unknown and uncertain space; leaving the religion I had grown up with and which my community followed, while not yet having found anything to replace it. This continued for many years. Music was perhaps the main focus of my new identity. In between the religion I had left behind and the faith I would one day find, there was music to fill the void. Morally, I called this period my "dark ages." Much of my life was guided by what I felt like doing or could get away with. And yet, in other ways, I was developing my values which were based on justice, equality, fairness, rule of law and inclusivity.

I did occasionally come across white people who were Christians and who were involved in some of the projects I was associated with. There was a project near where we lived called *All Faiths, One World*. Its leader used to wear a clerical collar, commonly known as a 'dog-collar.' There was another project in the building of a church where people could go to for advice on welfare matters. It was quite a strange project, I thought. The vicar of the church was white and most of the church congregation were black people, against whom Pakistanis are usually prejudiced on grounds of their colour. Most, if not all, of the staff who worked at the centre were Muslim, either Pakistani or Bangladeshi. What was particularly significant was that most of the users of the centre's services were from the local Pakistani community. The centre had an excellent reputation and people appreciated its professional service which was offered free of charge. Whether you were a *miraasi*, low caste, or a *raja*, high caste, you were treated the same. The community especially appreciated the fact the centre offered a confidential service. One could take any problem to the staff and they would deal with it as best they could but would never disclose the details to anyone else. So secrets stayed secret. Pakistani women also felt welcome in the centre, which was more than could be said about similar facilities offered by their own community. For me, this presented a real challenge. What does 'community' mean in such a situation? We have a phrase in Urdu, *apney loag*, our own people. Who was this meant to be; the Christian vicar who oversaw the project, the Bangladeshi project leader or the black church members whose funds paid for the centre?

Another key change which had taken place in my attitude was that, unlike many of my community, who think home is in Pakistan or they are not sure where it is, I was very definite that I was not going 'back home' as the phrase goes. I was already at home in England. As soon as I started work, I paid into the funds of the *Death Kameti* which had been set up by our village and continued for a few years. Its purpose was to help members meet expenses related to death such as paying for the deceased to be transported back to Pakistan. In addition, the expenses of one or two close relatives accompanying the body would also be met.

Having already decided to stay away from the general *kameti* system, I now decided to discontinue my involvement in the *Death Kameti*.

This 'burning of bridges' was later reinforced when I decided against having a dual nationality, which would have enabled me to be a national of both UK and Pakistan. For me, there was only one home, only one country for which I would live (there was no need to die for it) and do whatever I could to make it a better place.

When my parents sent me to England, what were they thinking? What did they expect to achieve? They had many children, all of whom except me were girls. According to the culture they knew all the girls were only temporary members of the family. One by one, each would, through marriage, leave and become part of someone else's family. So, I was the only son, their only insurance for old age. They didn't need to articulate this; in their world this was how things were and how they had always been. They had brought me up lovingly. I was their prince. I was their future. They knew I would look after them in their old age.

Although at the time they had not articulated their thoughts and desires for me, these had slowly become clear. I knew they expected me to have a good future. What did this mean? I know my father wanted me to carry on with my education, building on what had been started in the village. The rest I had to develop myself, and did so quite successfully. I had gotten myself a job, a good job, and now I owned my own house, which was no mean achievement for a twenty year-old. Since leaving school four years prior, I had continued my education in the evenings and through my day-release study. I knew that in another two years I would have enough qualifications—five O Levels and two A Levels—to go to university. But I had achieved much more during these eight years.

I had not just made England my home; I had fallen in love with the place and its ways. I loved its weather. Where else can you start a conversation with a complete stranger about how good or bad the weather has been? Where else can you stand in a queue and be served when it is your turn without a question being asked as to whose son you are, which village you are from, or how much you are willing to pay even if the service is meant to be free. If you need an official document, you complete a form and put in the post and wait, knowing that in due course you will get what you have applied for. Or you post something, even valuable things, knowing that it would get there without someone intercepting it and taking out the contents of the letter or the parcel. These may be little things for people who can take such minutiae for granted, but for those of us who are from cultures where we cannot, they are very significant. It is these little things that make life what it is.

There is a phrase they use in England to do with marriage; leave and cleave. It is where a person leaves his parents and cleaves to his or her new partner. This was exactly what had happened to me. I had left my parents and my country and had become united to England, my bride. I breathed a different kind of air. Little did I know then that the best was yet to come.

So, going to Pakistan for me was visiting my birthplace which had become a foreign place. As for my parents, they would be expecting me to come back home and pick up where I had left off.

2929 days later

Every time she cooked she had to light a fire. Except this time she was thinking of her boy. How he used to fetch her dry grasses and hay that she would put at the bottom of the *choola*, fireplace. She would then place the kindling which he had often gathered while out with the goats and add a few thicker sticks before lighting it with the *maatchuss*, matches. All the time he would stand there watching her. Later, he would come and sit with her on the little *piri*, stool, just on her left, and eat his roti. He said he liked the burning smell. She was always glad of his company.

It was going to be a long time before she and my father would see me again.

After seeing me off with my father on that autumn day, my dear mother busied herself with her chores. She cried while tending to her buffalo, while she went to fetch water from the well, while she cooked—even though she could not eat the food afterwards. She cried waiting for my father to return. When he didn't, she cried herself to sleep on her own. Her precious son had been taken from her; only Allah knew when she would see him again. She would see him again, wouldn't she?

She had never done this before and didn't know another woman whose son had gone off to a foreign place where they do things differently. How would he cope without her? Will he eat properly? Will it be roti or some strange food? Even if he did, she knew it would not be made of home-grown flour from their own family fields which had fed them for generations.

The next day, she woke up very early in the morning. She realised I was not there. Of course, I was not; she had allowed them to take me away to vilayat. She knew that while she was asleep she had forgotten that I had gone away. She felt guilty about this. How could she fail to think about her boy's absence? What sort of mother was she?

She milked the buffalo as usual. She always talked to the animal while doing so. Except this morning she began to cry as soon as she sat down on the piri seat, ready for the task ahead. She knew she should cook some breakfast but did not feel like it. How could she cook the *parathas*, butter roti, when her dear firstborn was not there to eat them as he did every morning before going off to school. Instead, she decided to re-heat the food she had cooked the night before and eat some of it. She kept feeling as if someone close had died. She had to remind herself that this was not the case. All that had happened was her son had gone to vilayat where he would have free education and then a good job. He would be able to send money home like all the other vilayati people. Then one day, he would return and get married. He would have a choice of girls. Would it be her sister's daughter who had not had any education? Or would it be that other girl he played with and who was also closely related? She might be a better choice. He was bound to pick her as she was very fair, almost a *gori*, like all the girls he would see in vilayat.

About lunch time, when she was thinking whether she could be bothered to cook, just for herself, she saw someone over the distant hill coming towards our village. Soon, she realised it was her dear husband. She could tell from his walk that it was him. Last time she had seen him, he was with her boy and now . . . .

He didn't say much when he reached home, other than that he had spent the night the other side of Dadyal, in some relatives' home. He had got near their house when it was getting dark and rather than walking home in the dark, he decided to stay with them.

She cooked lunch for them both and took his to the *baithak*, sitting room. He was sitting there, staring in space. She could see he had been crying too. Neither of them said anything. She went back to the *rasoi*, kitchen, to eat her food.

A few minutes later, my father walked into the rasoi with his food. He said he didn't want to eat on his own. Normally I would have eaten with him. After a few long minutes of silence, he began to talk about his trip to the airport.

He told her about me vomiting at the bus station in Mirpur and then falling asleep during most of the rest of the journey. He told her that he had bought me a bag of *naizay*, pine nuts, to take with me to vilayat. She said the nuts would not last that long; she knew they were my favourites. As she said it, for some reason she smiled. Perhaps, it was being able to picture me, something she was going to have to do quite a lot for the next few years.

Soon, it was evening. After having their meal and tending to the animals they settled down, ready to go to sleep. But then one of the neighbours arrived and then another and another. Before long, there were quite a few people, all women, who had turned up, knowing the family would need company. This time there was not the laughter and conversation full of stories as on my last night there. While this evening everyone was sitting inside, on that occasion there were so many people that they could not all be fitted inside; some of the latecomers had to sit outside in the dark. There were not enough *butti* lanterns to go round.

The conversation was subdued. It was obvious they were struggling to say anything worthwhile. Someone said something which reminded Ji about me. He suddenly decided it was bedtime. "Stop, nattering girls, it's time to go to sleep," So they all got up and went.

After they had gone, the lantern was turned off. It was silence, absolute silence and completely dark. Both of them lay there in their beds thinking. Bey cried. Did Ji cry? He could if he wanted to; there was no one around. More silence and dark. Both pretended to sleep, but really they were wide awake and thinking about what had happened to their family unit. One precious boy and they sent him away. How long will it be before they see him again? Will it be days, weeks, months or years? A year is a long time!

Neither felt like sharing their thoughts with the other. For now and on many other such occasions they would simply share their silence with each other. Except, occasionally, they would let out some sign that they were thinking about their boy.

The next day came and the day after that. Before long, a week had passed since my departure. So one or the other of the parents or visiting neighbour would say "It's a whole week since . . ." Another week passed. Before long it was a month since I had left. Then, it was the next season. It was time to prepare the fields for the next crop. Soon, it was harvest time. This was followed by another crop and another and another after that.

When I arrived home the first thing my mother said—after she had stopped crying—"it's been 71 less than 3000 days." Not having been to school, she didn't know how to say 2929 days. At first, I could not understand what she meant. But then one of the village boys explained. Apparently, with his help, during all the time I was away, she had worked out how many days it had been since she last saw me. The boy was good at maths. Like me, he had also come top in his class. I never did check whether their sums were right. But it did help me to realise that I had been away many days. Too many for my parents before they would hear my voice or look at me. Now, I both looked and sounded different.

I discovered that the clothes I left behind had not been thrown away. Mum explained that they reminded her about me. "For many months, they used to smell of you." She kept all my school text books and the few exercise and note books I had written on, though we mostly wrote on our *takhti* and slate and rubbed it off afterwards.

She told me that in the early days, every time they cooked chicken, she would remember me not being there to eat the giblets; who else deserved such a special treat? She similarly noticed my absence when someone said the *azaan*, call to prayer, or when they didn't say it. "If my son was here now he would say it," she thought to herself. Or if she was building her fire to cook on and needed kindling, which I used to fetch for her.

When she saw my cousin come back from the big city where he had gone to college, she would say, or at least think, that if her boy had not gone away he would be at the big school and would also return like so.

Apparently, when my letters arrived she used to kiss them and ask my father to read them to her as she could not read Urdu. Just like a child who wants to hear stories again and again, she used to ask my father to read my letters to her many times over. And when he wasn't around or when she thought he had got fed up reading them to her, she used to ask one of the village boys who had been to school to read her the letters.

In the early days she used to dread going to weddings. The women there used to ask her if she had had a letter from me. She would get fed up with such questions. But later these gatherings were a trigger for a different script. Once, when I had left school and was earning, my father wrote in one of his letters that whenever my mother comes back from having attended a wedding, she says, "One day my boy will come back and we will have a big wedding, the biggest. We will invite everyone in the village and more. It will be the biggest and best gathering; after all we only have one son. It's not as if we will have that chance again."

I wasn't able to gather any more stories about life for my parents during those eight or so years of my absence. Neither of them wanted to talk about what must have been a painful period in their lives. It was only many years later when I had become a parent myself that I began to get an inkling what it must have been like for them without me there as a part of their lives.

One of the village ladies explained to me that every time a local person had come back from England, my mother would visit them to find out if they had any news of me and would send her love with them if they were returning there. And if it was a woman who was going to England, then she would give them a couple of extra kisses for them to pass onto her boy. Sometime she would begin to cry then stop and say, "Don't tell my son."

Des or perdes!

By this time it was eight years since I left my parents. I had not spoken to them during this time except for the odd letter exchanged.

My parents thought they knew all about me. They had heard about me from relatives. They knew what I had been upto. Through my letters and tapes I had sent and words from visiting relatives who had met me, met someone who had met me or who had seen me or thought they had seen me, my parents had been able to form a picture about me, who I was and what I had been upto. I was amazed at the detail my parents had had about my life. They would tell me about some man who had come to see me for help with some official form he needed filling and I had been very helpful. Or someone who had come to see me but I had pretended I was not in. "He must have been wrong." My parents could not believe that I would be so inhospitable. Someone even told them that I was spotted going into a pub, an English butchers (surely they don't sell halal food which Muslims are supposed to eat), holding hands with a *gori*, white girl. Apparently, someone had come up to me when at a big public meeting or event I had organised and I had pretended not to recognise the person who was a close relative.

I had a vague recollection of some of it. I could not work out the timing of some of what they had heard. It was all a big jumble.

There is a Punjabi phrase *des, perdes*, home and away, our own country and abroad. It is linked to the saying *apney, pariay*, us and them or our

106

own people and foreigners. The trouble was that for me and my parents our *des, perdes* was the opposite way around. While they thought that I had come home from a foreign country, for me, being in Pakistan where I had grown up and had a very happy childhood and where all my early friendships had been formed was now the foreign place.

Above all else, I had decided that Britain was my home now and its ways of doing things were my ways. At times it had begun to feel as if its heritage was now my heritage. I did not know at the time but one day the country's religious heritage would also become mine. The civilisation I was surrounded by—the democracy, the culture, and the values—had not happened overnight but had taken centuries to develop. All the struggles that had gone into making the country what it was had, as a British citizen, become my struggles. Sadly, this was not how many of my fellow Pakistani migrants felt. For them, being in the West was temporary and home was still Pakistan to which they would return one day. Will this change? Will there be a time when they start to think of England as home?

A few months before, just as I thought I had done everything to do with my trip, I had a letter from my father. This outlined what I should bring in terms of gifts and for whom. He explained that as a *vilayati* coming back for the first time, there were expectations. People knew that I was doing very well. "After all, you work in an office and get paid monthly, not like factory workers."

"Of course", he explained, "you have additional expectations on you because you are from *our family*." He reminded me of our family's status in the village. As *sufaid-poash* folk we had to keep up appearances. Even if we have no money, we behave as if we have. So he said if I don't have the money to buy all the gifts for people, I should borrow the money from my friends. "They won't mind," he said, "if you explain it to them." He also advised me that before I leave for Pakistan I must see all the family who live near me. This I did over the weekends and some evenings when I was not at evening school. Many of them gave me letters to take to their loved ones back home, some just verbal messages. Some also gave me presents. I took a few things but refused many because I did not want to be over the weight limit at the airport and have to pay a fee. Some relatives gave me pound notes to give to their families or some childhood friend. I decided to write it all down in case I forgot. One or two gave me photographs that had been taken properly at the photographers, looking very sombre and always sitting up with hands on their thighs.

The 'foreignness' of Pakistan was apparent as soon as I got on the plane, the Pakistan International Airlines. It was as if my fellow passengers had already arrived in their country of origin. They began to behave in a 'Pakistani' way. Interestingly, they were also being treated by the airline staff as if we were in Pakistan.

Upon arrival at Islamabad Airport, there was even more of an alien environment. The customs staff expected to be bribed. Of course, they didn't say so. It was just obvious from their behaviour. So I gave them a few pounds. Although the officer took it from me, he was muttering that it wasn't enough and he called me a *kanjoos*, Urdu for miser. I thought to myself, "What a world I have come to?"

I also had to battle it out with the porters. They were supposed to be there to serve us but compared to what I had been used to in England, this was not service. They were so aggressive and pushy.

After clearing customs, I came out. There was a sea of people who were just staring at us. I thought, "How am I going to find my father amongst this mass of people?" Fortunately, he saw me just as I came out. He had already arranged a taxi for us for the long journey to the village. It took us nearly the whole day to get to our destination. We went through a number of places which I had heard of or remembered them from my journey to England all those years ago; Gujar Khan, Dina, passing the dam at Mangla and then through New Mirpur and Plaak before arriving in Dadyal and onwards towards our village. We arrived in Lalpur and stopped to have a break in someone's house. We then left my luggage there, because the rest of the journey was about an hour's walk.

We were still some distance away from our village, but I could see the houses. I could just about make out one or two people. Was it my mother? "It is not long now, before I see her," I thought to myself. By the time we reached home, it seemed the whole village had arrived to greet me. My dear mother would not stop kissing me. She was crying at the same time and got me started too. A few of the other women came and kissed me on the cheeks. The men would hug me in the special way that people did when they saw someone after a long time, especially if they had come from England.

All the adults were congratulating my parents, "Mubarak ji." With young children, I would just shake their hands. The very little ones, too shy to come forward to greet me, were being pressured by their mothers or older sisters to shake my hand.

When I had finished greeting everyone, I was advised to change since I was still in my western clothes, of shirt and trousers. The right clothes to wear now were *kameez, shalwar.* They had a set made for me. I went inside and changed.

While changing my clothes, I noticed that my school photo was on the mantelpiece. This was the one where I was wearing my prefect badge. My parents thought this was such an honour. Apparently, they would mention it to everyone who would enquire about me in those early days. I might have gone across the 'seven seas', but I was still their son. They were proud of my achievements. Maybe one day I would send them a photo of me receiving a degree, wearing one of those silly black hats and gowns.

The room had changed little since I was here as a child. The cupboards still had my text books. The walls had new hangings, the kind that are typical in Muslim houses. One was a picture of the *Kaaba,* the black stone in Mecca that Muslims face when praying and the other said Allah and Muhammad (peace be upon him).

After the evening meal—my mother's special chicken curry, with home grown chicken and roti—I was advised to take a brief rest. I was told that visitors would start coming. I thought they had been already but what I had not realised was the earlier visitors were just the immediate neighbours. A little while after the evening we would have visitors from the wider village. Also, this time they would come for longer.

They did come, lots of them. I don't know how many exactly but the house was full. The *baithak,* sitting room, was full of men, sitting on the *khat* or *charpoy,* bed. The women and girls were all in the next room. At first the young boys were sitting with us men but then when the room began to fill up they had to go outside, giving up their seats to older men. The really young boys were just hanging around wherever they could find space. They were free to go either with the men or with the women.

Soon, it began to go dark so the *butti,* lanterns were lit. One was placed in our room, one in the other room with the women and one outside in the courtyard. Later, one of the neighbours came with a *gas.* This was a bigger lantern, probably the equivalent of four or five *buttis.* I think it was called 'gas' because it made a hissing sound when it was on, like a gas cooker in England.

Whenever anyone came who had not been already, they would greet me in the same way, with the three hugs and a handshake. Returning visitors would simply arrive with a *salaam-alaikum* greeting and shake hands. As I had seen amongst my family in England, whenever there is a group of people, if you shake hands with one person you should shake hands with everyone. Otherwise they would be offended.

People would come and ask me how I was, say *Mubarak* to my parents and ask me how their relatives were in England. Sometime, my father would rescue me by saying that I had been busy with my studies and had not been able to see everyone before leaving for Pakistan or that I was too tired to talk. On one occasion, I told someone I had something for them that their family had given me in England but it was quickly pointed out that there was no hurry. "We will see you again, many times, before you go back. There is no hurry."

The conversation would start again. One person, usually my father, would talk and the others would listen. The conversation would be about anything that had happened in the village or some story from elsewhere.

I was so impressed with my father to be able to talk so authoritatively. I could not imagine doing anything like it. While in England, I had maintained my Urdu to a point. In some ways I had a wider vocabulary than when I left Pakistan. Although I could just about hold a one-to-one conversation, I would not be able to speak in front of so many people. It was made particularly difficult as the conversation had to be conducted in our local dialect which I used very little in England as I had moved away from my community.

After a little while, some of the women began to make tea on the *choolah*, open fire. This was seen as a treat by the visitors, many of whom would not have milk at home to make the tea. The tea was served in china cups and saucers. These would normally be stored on the high shelf near the ceiling, on show to everyone.

By the time every one of the forty or fifty people had been served tea, the evening would begin to come to a close. Slowly, people would start to leave with their *buttis*. One or two had brought *batteries*, the local word for torch.

Then we began to get ready to go to sleep. I was not looking forward to this part. I was used to sleeping in my own bed, in my own separate room, with privacy. Here, I was going to be sleeping with my father on the other bed. I had got used to running water. Sometimes, I liked to have a bath before bed. More than anything, I was used to having a toilet in my house. Here, they still had to rely on the fields for that. How would I cope in the dark? I was afraid of it ever since my childhood, hearing all those ghost stories. Worse still, how would I cope in the morning when others would be able to see me in the open fields? Would I be able to find a secluded spot or a bush to hide behind? I had got used to having toilet paper; how would I cope with stones or bits of soil to wipe my bottom?

The following morning, I was woken by the *azaan*, call to prayer. My father woke up, did his ablutions with the warm water my mother had got and heated for him. I pretended to still be asleep. I had stopped saying my prayers and didn't want my father to find out. My plan was to avoid going to the village *masjid*, mosque. But, if that didn't work then I would go with someone and follow their steps while pretending I knew how to pray. It wouldn't look good for people to find out that I could not pray properly. They would talk about it forever and it would bring such shame on our family. I guess it was my own fault to be so goody-goody as a child. If I had been like the other children I would never have known how to pray in the first place.

A couple of days later, I went to pray. I managed to remember how to do it. When to stand, how to fold my arms in the correct manner, sit, prostrate, it all came back as if it was second nature. However, I refused to call the azaan. My mother so wanted me to stand in the courtyard of the mosque and call out to everyone so she could say "Just like you used to when you were little." I think she wanted everyone to know that her little boy was back and life was as it used to be.

I did manage to find a secluded spot in our field near the house to do my 'business. When I came back to the house, I was given warm water so I could have a wash in the little cubicle they had built, adjoining the house.

We then had breakfast, of tea and *parathay*, buttered roti.

I changed out of my kurta pyjama that I had slept in, back into my kameez shalwar. We knew that any minute now visitors would start to arrive. We were right. However, it wasn't so much visitors but musicians. I remembered from my childhood the family of artisans in our village who used to play the bagpipes and the *dholki* drum. They had turned up given it was a special occasion. They were accompanied by one of their children who did a dance. After a few minutes, I was asked to give them some money. I had brought some Pakistani rupees with me from England. My mum gave me some as well. The artists were given some tea.

We then began to have visitors. This was to continue for the rest of the day and into the evening. Some of them had already been the day before while others were making their first visit. They would stay for a while, ask me how I had been, comment on how I had changed, enquire about their loved ones in England and then get into some conversation, about anything. They were offered tea.

At around mid-day we ate our lunch. Most visitors had disappeared, as if by magic. It was curry from the previous night with fresh roti which had just been made on the *tawa*, griddle. I ate it with my father, separate from the women.

As soon as I finished my lunch, I had to go and pay my respects to a number of the families who had had a death during my years in England. My mother pointed out whose house to go to and reminded me who had died. I visited six families. At each, I would arrive and they would know who I was and why I had come. I would say *afsose*, in other words, I am sorry about the deceased. After some polite conversation, I would lift my hands in prayer and say *Fatihah*, first surah of the Quran, in Arabic. The man of the house, if there was one, would join me. The women just watched. I could just about remember how to say the *Fatihah* from my childhood. In any case, it didn't matter if I hadn't since I was saying it quietly. So, for all they knew I could be just moving my lips. The same could equally be said of the host. I would then move to the next house and do the same. Although, I was offered a cup of tea, my mother had said I was not to accept since it would take too long. In any case, if you have tea in one house and not the next, it would be bad politics.

During this first walk around my village, I could see it had changed. There were quite a few more houses. In fact, on one occasion I had to ask for directions to one of the houses I visited. It was obvious which houses were *vilayati,* made with English money. They were the ones made with brick as opposed to local stone. Two or three looked as if they had been built in the past couple of years. One even had a gate so visitors had to knock and wait to be let in. This was very novel, very city like. The new houses also had the facility for electricity and running water, both of which were imminent, I was told.

When I came back, my cousins had arrived from Siakh, near the dam. Some of their family had to relocate when the dam was first built. They had walked for about three hours. I got the impression they would stay the night. My dad killed two chickens while I stood there watching him; some things don't change!

The conversation began to include references to how long I was staying. People began to say that three weeks was not enough and that I should stay at least six months.

By the end of the second day, people began to enquire when the *Big Day* was, meaning wedding. At first, I thought it was none of their business when I would get married. I would do it when I was ready. But I soon realised that this *was* their business. They had waited for me to come back and get married so they could have a bit of fun, wear their finest clothes and eat special food.

The word got out that I did not want to get married. What sort of response was that! Why wouldn't I want to get married! I had grown up, I had a good future, with a respectable office job. I even lived in my own house. Of course, it was natural that I should get married; everyone said so in one way or another. Even when they did not say it, I knew they were thinking it.

After a couple of days, the subject of my marriage was all around me. Most of the time my parents did not say anything. If someone tried to draw them into the subject, they would mutter something such as, "We've asked him and he says no." But it was a different matter altogether when I was alone with them. This happened at night, after all the visitors had gone to their homes. We would switch off the lantern and lie in complete darkness. They would try all sorts of tricks to persuade me; how lovely the girls were, I could choose whichever one I fancied; who would look after them in their old age, it was my religious duty to make sure my parents are looked after; I just had to get engaged and may be get married next time. They even said to me that I could have two wives. I just had to get married in the village and was free to do whatever I wanted in England. I stuck to my guns. I made my views clear. I did not want to get married. Having said so a number of times, sometimes I just said nothing. They knew my silence was a 'no.'

The situation was not helped by the fact that each and every one of the boys my age who were at school with me were already married and, in most cases, had a number of children.

My family also tried to find out if there was a girl in England who I fancied. I wish there had been. I could then give them an explanation. Mind you, it would have been different kind of battle, not necessarily easier.

After a while, I began to dread being on my own with my parents. I knew what they would say. They talked about nothing else. From time to time, my mother would start to cry. My father would use that as moral blackmail. I still wasn't budging. Sometimes, I would get up and go for a walk. I found this helped me to gather my thoughts and get back in touch with my own reality; who I was, what my aspirations were, where I belonged and where I needed to get back to soon.

Occasionally, I had to go with my father to visit someone in another village. Of course, we walked there. As tradition would have it, I walked behind him. In some ways this helped as he could not eyeball me. I learned to manage conversations in order to steer away from the dreaded subject of marriage.

During these times, I realised that my birthplace was actually a very beautiful part of the world. I didn't notice this when I was here during my early years. Then it felt like an ordinary place. Having been away, I noticed its beauty. While in England, I had been to Wales quite a few times; it so reminded me of home. I had also been to Cornwall. The sea was a new experience for me, shame it was so cold to swim in. I used to look at the open space at the many beaches and imagine playing kabaddi there with my mates. Once, I also went to Scotland and saw its mountains and lakes. And, of course, there was the beauty of the urban world around me. But, now I was able to be a tourist in my birthplace. People thought it was odd that I was taking photographs. "What's so special about this place when you've come from England where they have everything!"

As a child, I had come across cigarettes even though I was not allowed to smoke. I remembered one of the brands was called K2. I now realised that this was the world's second tallest mountain and it was in Pakistan. I also had discovered that Kashmir had been described as 'heaven on earth' and Switzerland of the East.

After a few days in the village, England seemed so far. At times it felt as if it hadn't happened. Did I just imagine it! What England, where, who . . . There were momentary lapses when I would enter my parents' world. Their norms would become mine, however briefly. I would then think, "Maybe I should get married. It would certainly make things easier." There would be a big party. Everyone would come in their best clothes. I would go to my in-laws and come back with a bride. After four days, she would go back to her parents. She would then return and settle down in her new home. She would be our responsibility. She would belong to us. Her *izzat* would be our *izzat*. We would have children and live happily ever after.

I would then wake up and realise that this was not what I had planned to do. I was going to marry a woman of my own choosing. She would be an equal partner in my life. She would not be subservient to me.

It helped that before going to Pakistan I had articulated my intentions to a number of friends. This rehearsal was helpful now. It became my script in response to my family's demands. But it was hard. It was as if the whole world was asking me to do one thing and I wanted the exact opposite. It was one thing sharing my intentions with my friends in England; sticking by them here was another matter altogether.

I began to count the days until my departure. I planned to spend some time away visiting the big city. I pretended that I had to write an article on immigration. This was a bit of wishful thinking on my part. I had pretensions to be a journalist by then, having written a few articles for the Urdu press. I fancied writing something for New Society. So I arranged to go to Islamabad.

I managed to explore parts of the country I had heard of before but never seen. It reinforced for me that I was in a foreign country. On one occasion, I needed to ask for directions. Back home in England, I had learnt that you can always ask a police man for directions, which is the opposite of what they do in Pakistan. Here, a police man would be the last person you would go to. So, when I walked into a police station and asked for directions, it was probably the first time anyone had come into their building voluntarily to ask for help.

Also, during the trip, I learnt that they don't queue here. I was in some government offices to get a document. After waiting a long time, I realised that there were people coming after me but being served before me. I concluded that anyone of any status did not queue but was served straight way. I caused a bit of a fuss and was then served. I began to speak in English in order to be assertive. It helped because my English was better than the person serving me, as well as his manager.

When I came back from my travels, it was only a few days before I was due to go back to England. I had already been to the offices of Pakistan International Airlines to confirm my seat. There was an acceptance, a resignation, by my parents that my marriage was not to be.

I spent the remaining few days packing my belongings. I had bought a whole suitcase full of Urdu books by authors I had heard of. There were a large number of books by Manto.

As a part of my goodbye, I visited all the families in the village, going to each house for a few minutes. One or two would say things such as, "So you are going back," meaning, "There is no marriage then, no wedding celebrations."

In the evenings, we began to have visitors at home. It was a repeat of what had happened at the start of my time there. People came to see me, to give me letters, messages and gifts for their loved ones in England. Occasionally, someone would bring up the subject of my marriage. They would soon be told to be quiet by my father. He had had enough of the subject.

Then, I was at the airport, safely through all the checks. I was on my way home. I was pleased, and very lucky, to have parents who had some decency about them. They tried every which way to persuade me to get married or engaged but did not go beyond words. I was at their mercy and that of the wider community. They did not take my passport away. Had they done that, I would not have been able to turn to anyone for help since, according to their norms, I was in the wrong. There would have been no point to make reference to my human rights. Such things only had meaning in the political and cultural context of a place far away. In any case, the law would not have been there to enforce it. Had it become involved, it would have sided with my parents.

Sadly, just as I was about to board the plane, I was reminded how my community was perceived by the rest of Pakistanis. I heard the airline man telling the old man before me to hurry up, otherwise the plane might go without him. The old man started to run. The official then turned to me and said, "These Mirpuris, they are so simple." He had a chuckle. I was wearing my three-piece pinstripe suit. So he must have thought I was some sophisticated city person. When I pointed out that I was also a Mirpuri, he became embarrassed and quickly processed me.

I arrived at Heathrow Airport, joined the queue for people with British passports and was allowed through without any questions. I collected my luggage and was soon on the coach home. I was back in my own world where they do things differently.

The visit was enlightening as it helped me to understand myself. More than anything, it was clear to me that I was not one for doing anything against my will. It was preparation for me to go against the grain in other situations. Little did I realise what was coming my way.

She's the one

Back in the safety of the world that had now become my home, I worked hard. Alongside my job, I continued to attend evening classes and day-release at college. I was now studying my A Levels. I needed two for the degree course I was aiming for. I already had my five O Levels. I was now employed as a Community Worker, which involved working mainly with my own local community. But as it was only for two years. I needed to get to university at the end of it. During the first year of my A Level course, I very badly failed one of the subjects. Someone suggested that I could use my Urdu since I was fluent in it. So I did. I managed to get my second A Level in the subject and satisfy the university entrance requirements.

I was now ready to go to university. It felt such a privilege to be amongst my fellow students. I was the first in my family and community to go to university, especially as a first generation immigrant. I could not believe that I had the luxury of being able to study for three whole years. And, as a mature student, I qualified to receive a grant.

I don't think most people had any idea how long my journey had been to get to this point and all that it had involved. Mind you, I could barely take it in myself. I rented out my house and moved into university accommodation. After three years, I would be able to send my parents another photograph, of me holding my degree certificate. It would have pride of place on their mantelpiece, next to my other photo. But what I did not realize was that I would leave university with much more than a degree. My life was going to radically change during those three years in ways beyond my wildest dreams.

During the first few weeks I got involved in student life. I had heard that students spend most of their time having fun. I tried to do the same. But thankfully I soon settled down to doing what I was there to do; study. Not surprisingly, I was a conscientious student.

I took my study seriously. I focused on getting my degree and all the opportunities it would bring for me. As before, I approached the situation incrementally, one assignment and module of study at a time. I attended every lecture and worked diligently on every assignment I was set. I could not believe my luck when I realised the college I was attending had its own library. I could read as many of its books and journals as I wanted to.

At a personal level, I had spent ten long years as a little boy lost in the wilderness. This was about to change. I fell in love! Linda was a final year student. There was a real intellectual connection between us and much more besides. I instantly knew that 'she is the one' after one of my favourite songs. I now understood what my friends had meant that I would know when I met the right girl. We soon became engaged.

When I first met her family, I was struck by the fact that they had her elderly grandmother living with them; they had built an extension to their house in order to accommodate her. This had a major impact on me as it challenged my stereotypes of white people. I had been brought up believing that white people put their elders in old people's homes.

Suffice to say, our relationship was not what either of our families had in mind for us. But the more opposition we faced the more determined we were.

Linda was already a Christian. She had become a Christian in her teens, the first Christian in her family. Here, I learnt what being a 'born-again Christian' meant. It wasn't about being born into a religion but actually making a conscious decision. I wondered why someone like her was getting mixed up with me. I was to understand later that the Lord moves in mysterious ways. If we hadn't met then, my life would have taken a very different course. Mind you, I would be leading a very different life if lots of things hadn't happened in my past.

While at university, I learned something about Christianity, both good and bad. There were plenty of Christians telling me that following Christ was the only way to get to heaven, and that everyone else was destined for the fires of hell. Some of this actually encouraged me to dig deeper into the religion of my birth and claim my links to it, but only superficially. When I was honest with people, I would admit that I wasn't a good Muslim or that I did not practice my religion. To do this when surrounded by lots of Christians took a level of courage and honesty. It would have been very tempting to claim that they had their religion and I had mine.

I also discovered another side of Christianity. I noticed that some of its followers stood out in their caring, welcoming and inclusive attitude generally, and towards outsiders like me. One evening, one of the colleges near our campus had invited a visiting Christian speaker. He was black. Most of his audience were white. As if this was not radical enough, he proceeded to talk about forgiveness and its active nature. He said it wasn't sufficient just *saying* sorry; one had to *do* sorry as well. This had a major impact on me. In the world I was familiar with, certainly in my own culture and community, there was often talk of revenge but rarely forgiveness.

At the end of the three years, I succeeded at achieving my degree qualification. Now, my parents would be able to show off a new photograph to their visitors and relatives. I could imagine my father telling everyone "He has a Bachelor of Education degree." He would use the English for added effect. He would remind everyone that I was the first, not just in our immediate family or in the village but in the whole extended family to achieve such a qualification. He would talk about how he had worried when first sending me to England in case my education would come to an end. Of course, through hard work and all the evening classes, I had managed to continue my education and get on to a degree course. "And all this on top of having a white-collar job and buying his own house". I wondered whether this would, partly, make up for the fact that I had gone against tradition and married a white woman.

Having given ourselves and our families a couple of years to get used to our relationship, we got married.

If I had followed the traditions of my community, where a few men had married white women, I would have expected my wife-to-be to accept my religion even though this was often just a formality. She would take on a Pakistani name, start wearing Pakistani clothes (the *shalwar kameez),* and generally start behaving like a Pakistani woman—sitting separately from the men when visitors came or walking behind me when out and about.

But given that I had moved away from the religion I was born into and my wife had an active faith, some of which I found appealing, I agreed to get married in a Christian ceremony. In front of our friends and some of my wife's family, I declared:

> *I take you to be my wife. To have and to hold from this day forward, for better, for worse, for richer, for poorer, in sickness and in health, to love and to cherish till death do us part, according to God's holy law; and this is my solemn vow.*

Linda made a similar declaration.

We exchanged rings and signed the wedding register in front of witnesses. We were now man and wife. We then went and had a meal at a nearby restaurant before going off on our honeymoon for a few days.

Most couples would now start their living happy-ever-after, but not us!

My parents directly or indirectly, through all the relatives, continued to oppose my marriage. However, they still continued to be civil to her. The best example of this was when after a few years of our marriage we both went to visit them in Pakistan. My father said, "I took one look at her and decided that she is also someone's daughter." From this moment onwards, he treated her as if she was his own.

Throughout these years of struggle about my choice of wife, I knew that I could have made my life easier. I could have gone to Pakistan and married a girl of my family's choosing. I could have left her there to look after my parents and come back to England and lived normally. But this was not me. I had made my choice and that was that. I was not about to take a second wife just for an easy life.

In the same way, I could have made life easier for us both if my wife had become a Muslim, taken a Pakistani name and worn *kameez shalwar*. But I was not for taking the easy option.

Soon after our big day, we began to get reaction from my family to the decision I had taken. It started with a letter from my father which pointed out that by marrying a non-Muslim I was going to lose my *imaan*, my belief. Furthermore, our children would be non-Muslim. Unbeknown to him, this turned out to be quite a prophetic statement. He went on to advise that I must seek out a Muslim wife. "There are bound to be Muslim girls in England," he said. On the other hand, if I must marry an English girl then I must only do so after she has accepted Islam. In such a case, I must also be prepared to get married to a local village girl so she can look after her in-laws in their old age.

When that approach did not work, my father wrote another letter. Now I was being advised to gather together a few respectable people from the community, meaning the Muslim/Pakistani community, who would act as witnesses so we could marry according to Islamic rules. He stressed that I must then proceed to teach my wife all the essentials of Islam. He further asked me to write to him to let him know once I had followed his advice. Suffice it to say, his advice was ignored. From my point of view, I was already married and that was the end of that.

When he saw his advice being ignored, my father wrote to me asking to send to them my wife's size so they could send her some Pakistani clothes. I think they must have thought that at least this way she would wear some proper clothes, none of the foreign and strange clothes English women wear. After all, some of them don't even cover their legs. In this letter, I was also advised to give my wife a Pakistani name. They even suggested a name we could use. I was given another reminder that it was my duty as a Muslim to teach her about my religion.

Around this time, I received a letter from my 'special' teacher at secondary school. He had heard the news from my father and had decided to write to persuade me to reconsider my decision. What he and others like him did not appreciate was that I was no longer a child. I was an adult who had survived and at times thrived since being sent away to England. I had become my own man. I was independently minded, determined to do my own thing and had the courage to be the odd one out and go against the grain of my family and community. Above all else, I was living in my own house, eating my own food and living a life I had shaped for myself. The time was well and truly gone when I might have toed the line of tradition.

And yet, in all the unpleasantness that surrounded us as a newly married couple, every now and then we would catch a glimpse of another, gentler and more loving side of my family. This was especially the case in relation to my mother and sisters. We even came to appreciate my stepmother around this time. She lived in our second family home, many miles away from where my own mother lived. She wrote a letter—it will have been written by someone for her given that, like the other women in our family, she could not read or write—in which she congratulated us on our wedding and welcomed my wife to our family.

My sisters asked us to send them Linda's size so they could send her clothes. I knew this was different from what my father was talking about. For them, this is what they would have done towards any woman I had married. She would be their special *bhabi*, brother's wife. Of course, they wanted to shower her with gifts. At this point, I felt guilty that I had deprived them of a wedding in the village, with all the celebration activity which would go with it.

Soon after, I began to hear about the weddings of the girls who were my possible brides. Their parents had realised that I was no longer a 'prospect' for their daughters. One or two of these families had sent their representatives to visit us in our house to make sure that I was genuinely out of the picture as a son-in-law.

While all this was going on, I kept in regular contact with my parents, through letter and the occasional tape-recording. I rarely sent them letters or messages through fellow Pakistanis who were going back.

In my letters I would try to write about what was going on in our country which would mean something to my parents, especially my father. Most of my letters were written with him in mind. I remember writing to him about the first Pakistani Mayor in England. This was a historical moment for us generally but for me it had a particular interest. I had a fascination with Pakistanis who had come to England during the period my father had been here. It couldn't get any better than this because the man who had just become Lord Mayor of Bradford, Mohammed Ajeeb, had come to England in the same year as my father, in 1957. He also came from Tehsil Dadyal, the village of Chutrow, near to where our relatives lived. The 'mayor-making' ceremony was reported in all the Urdu newspapers; we had quite a few such papers by this time. Later, I would learn something of the history of the Pakistani community in England from the book which had been produced by Bradford Council. It had been compiled by Yaqub Nizami. This would confirm what I had learnt from my father about his time in the country. Mohammed Ajeeb in many ways was like my father—similar age, educated, respected and decent and with a positive outlook on life.

We began to get letters inviting us both to go to Pakistan so they could see my bride. This was a reminder for me that my family still loved me in spite of all that had happened.

We saved up and managed to go to Pakistan together a few years after getting married. All the members of my family were lovely, as were the people of the wider community, in how they received my new bride, their collective daughter-in-law. My parents did everything they could to make the house comfortable for us as a couple. They knew their daughter-in-law had been used to many comforts and did not want her to go without the essentials.

Seeing us together as a couple began to drive home the message to my family that we were indeed married and there was no other way.

A few years after this, we arranged for my mum and dad to visit us in England and see us in our own world. Now they were able to meet my in-laws who made my parents most welcome. For a couple who had not desired a Pakistani son-in-law, they went to great lengths to make my parents' visit enjoyable.

Knowing that their visitors were Muslims, they went out of their way to buy halal meat from a Pakistani shop in a part of town they would not normally frequent. While there, they managed to strike up a conversation with the shop-keeper and tell him about me, given that he had come from our district.

It was great to see both sets of parents together. The fact that they did not have a common language did not hinder their connection. I was able to interpret for them. At times, it felt like one of those important diplomatic situations where heads of two important states meet together and communicate with the help of interpreters. Our parents, I guess, were our heads of state.

While in England, my father visited both our workplaces. He was just about able to comprehend his daughter-in-law going out to work—he understood that it's normal for white people to send their women to work—but he found it really revolutionary that I had white people reporting to me. From having spent five years in England in the 1950s, he saw white people as the bosses, not as being managed by an immigrant from Pakistan. He saw this as a sign of real success and it seemed he would talk about it forever.

I was able to tell my father about my hero, Nelson Mandela. The year was 1988. A concert had been organised for him in London to draw the world's attention to his 25 years in prison. I remember sitting in our living room enjoying the music with my father and explaining to him who Mandela was.

Two years later, I sat in the same room to watch Mandela's release from prison. With tears of joy, I remember writing to tell my father about this momentous occasion.

It was to be a slow, very slow, process but my parents would finally come to terms with my choices. They would come to see, in my wife, a dedicated and loyal member of the family, one who had brought their son much happiness and wholeness. Still, who would have thought then that, one day, one of my sisters would refer to ours as a model marriage?

Nearly there!

My faith journey continued. We were living at my house, in a mainly Pakistani area. It was quite an oppressive environment. We had little freedom of movement. It was difficult to do much without it spreading through the community and beyond, even reaching my parents back in Pakistan. In some parts of our community, it felt as if our whole village from Dadyal had re-located to the UK, given that I was surrounded by so many of my relatives. Their gaze would be everywhere.

We were also living with constant pressure from an endless stream of relatives trying to persuade me to ditch my wife and get married to a girl in the family. Almost as soon as I told my parents of my relationship with an English girl, people amongst my family in England knew about it. I hadn't appreciated just how close the two countries were.

We had a stream of relatives visit us. At first, we had visits from male relatives of the girls (cousins mainly) whom I was supposed to have married. They were trying to confirm that what they had been told had indeed happened.

Many of these male visitors had come across white women in the workplace or in official situations. So they knew how to communicate with them with 'Yes miss, 'no miss.' Only on very rare occasions had they come across white women in a home environment. These were women who had 'married' into the community. Generally, they would behave as if they were Pakistani, since they had become 'Muslim.' They would dress in *kameez, shalwar* and speak broken Urdu, and sometimes they had a Pakistani name.

The trouble was that we saw things differently. Linda and I believed in equality between the sexes. We thought there was nothing wrong with her being in the same room as the men, as their equal. They found this very strange and probably threatening. Here was a woman, albeit white, in a family context who was refusing to take a subservient position to the men. It created a very uneasy environment and would completely disconcert the visitors. They would stay for a few minutes, have a drink—usually a cold drink since they would realize we would make 'English tea', which they would then decline—and then they would go. At this point, I would go with them to see them on their way. This gave them an opportunity to say anything they wanted to. During these brief moments I was offered a range of advice by the different men who had come. This included:

> *I should get rid of the gori, white woman and do as the culture required*

> *I should keep her in England and get married in Pakistan*

> *The gori should become a Muslim; she should at least wear 'our' clothes*

These visits continued for the next couple of years. At first, they were more intensive. Every weekend we would have men come to see us. Sometime, they were from the local area but at times they would travel many miles from other towns and cities. It was their duty to step in to my parents' role and put me on the straight path. But, gradually, word got out that I was not budging. I was determined to do what I wanted to and behave like a *gora*, white man. People then began to say that I was as stubborn as my own father. They would make reference to how he had refused to provide an alibi for a relative who had committed murder or how he had gone back home when everyone advised him to stay in England. Little did they realise that these conversations and stories actually encouraged me to stick to my guns and push against the community's rules and code. According to my way of seeing things, if my dear father could 'go against the grain' while still living amongst the community surely I could act according to my beliefs while living in my own house, eating my own *roti*. This was a free country, surely.

After a few years, we decided it was time to move house. We felt we deserved a little more distance between us and my relatives, somewhere we could have more space and freedom to be ourselves. We moved into a more 'white' area, a few miles away from where most of the Pakistanis lived. The mental distance that had begun to develop by this time between me and my family and community was now helped by the geographical and social distance. I also moved jobs to a nearby town. While still working with ethnic minority groups, the difference was that many of the people now were either Black Caribbean or Indian. This gave me a little more space to be me. I was allowed to work as a 'professional' instead of as a 'Pakistani,' which had been the case beforehand.

The separate life I had begun to lead soon after arrival in the UK and which had been given 'space' when I moved into my own house, now had a major boost. Away from the prying eyes of my relatives and fellow Pakistanis, I was able to associate more freely with a wider range of (white) people, including some Christians. This was to become even more significant later when, as active members of the church leadership, we began to use our house for Christian meetings. This would not have been possible in our previous location.

Linda started to attend a local church. I was generally happy with this but, occasionally, especially during some argument, I would complain that she was too involved in her church. "There is worship this, small group that and prayer the other; how much do you have to do, for goodness sake?" It was in part a worry that her faith would come between us. Yet at the same time, at least privately, I was pleased to be surrounded by this community of Christians.

This public-private tussle had gone on for many years. Around the time we were married, I remember I used to work with a man who wore a fish sign on his jacket lapel. I asked him what it was and he explained that it was a Christian symbol. Apparently, in the early days of the faith, when it was not safe to declare your faith to everyone, if a Christian met a stranger in the road, the Christian would draw one arc of the fish outline in the dirt. If the stranger drew the other arc, both would know they were followers of Christ. My colleague also had one of these symbols on his car. I recall that I looked for opportunities in our conversation to tell him about the fact that my wife was from his community of believers. Yet I know that, in those early days, publicly I was very far from joining the community myself.

During one trip to Pakistan, I had an interesting experience which showed me where I was on my faith journey at this time. I was with some friends, sightseeing in a big city some distance away from my parents' house. On one of the days, I noticed a church there. This was a first for me. I had not realized that, in our Muslim country, we had such buildings. In the grounds of the church, there were some people giving away free literature. I collected a few leaflets and a booklet; I liked freebies, especially literature. They also had a pile of Urdu books which they were selling. I bought one. The man had explained that it was the *injil*, New Testament. I had learnt by this time that Christians, Jews and Muslims, we were all *ehel-e-kitab*, people of the book. We all believed in the same prophets and in the same one God; not like the Hindus who had many gods. Linda was pleased to see me come back with an Urdu Bible.

I don't think I ever read my new book; to do so, would have been an admission that I was interested in a religion that was not mine. But, relationally, my faith journey was to continue.

I could see the Christians were a special group of people, different from any that I had encountered in all my time in England. They welcomed me, the stranger and outsider, into their fold. The significance of this can only be understood by appreciating what it means to be a minority, especially a visible minority such as the Pakistani community. Almost from day one of my arrival in England, it was clear to me that there was little in my culture and heritage that the white community appreciated. The fact that I could speak my mother tongue, write in Urdu and know a smattering of Farsi and Arabic did not count at all. I was told in no uncertain words that English was the only thing that mattered. The sooner I mastered it the better. Slowly, our food would be appreciated by the white community including by those who despised us. The irony was that there were people who would happily eat a curry, sometime with chips, and then go and abuse the people whose food it was. Even, and sometimes especially, people from our community working in restaurants would be treated with disdain by white customers.

I came across an article about virginity tests which Pakistani women were subjected to in the 1970s, upon arrival to the UK. It was to decide whether they were married. Why else would they come to England! The article was written by the Guardian journalist Huma Qureshi whose mother was one of the women who had suffered the humiliation. Fortunately, only 80 women were subjected to such a test before it was stopped. However, knowing it still leaves a nasty taste in the mouth. What other group would be treated in such an abusive manner and so recent in our past as well!

So, with this as a backdrop, to find white people who welcomed me into their fold meant a great deal.

While I am not into communities saying sorry their transgressions, I do wonder at times whether the majority community should do more to thank the Pakistani community for all they have contributed. Where would the 24/7 factories and foundries be without their hard work and willingness to work all hours for little money? Where would the National Health Service be without Pakistani doctors? What about the restaurants and much more besides? In fact, many of the areas in large towns and cities would no doubt be dead if it wasn't for the regeneration resulting from the Pakistani presence.

Soon after falling in love, I met one group of people who deserve a particular mention here. They were my Love's friends and family. Right from the start they made me feel at home. They gave me an opportunity to experience a white community, close up. They were able to offer me an alternative picture of their race and their community. I knew some of them were Christians. Even here, I was able to understand that not all Christians were the same. In time, I was to discover that, as ambassadors of their faith, this group was a lot closer to the One they were representing.

Later, I would meet Christians in my wife's church community who would slowly become my family. After being 'abandoned' by my parents while I was still a child, I thought I had perfected a way of managing on my own. Outwardly, I had a "I don't need anyone!" attitude, yet inwardly I longed for people who would look out for me, who would know my name, take the trouble to pronounce it properly, ask me about my family as if they genuinely wanted to hear it. I began to wonder if this was my new extended family, to take the place of the one I had left behind. They seemed to be the kind of people you would turn to and trust in times of need. It made me wonder whether they would provide for my children the supportive and loving environment that I had when I was growing up back in the village.

My journey continued.

Another nine years passed before I began to attend my wife's church. The arrival in our lives of our children was a growing-up process for me. After the birth of our daughter I became particularly keen that she should be brought up in an environment of equality, so she would grow up as a confident woman with all the opportunities available to men. After all, we were in a land where it was against the law to discriminate against women. The decision by me not to expect our daughter to be a Muslim was a clear indication of where I was on my faith journey. She did not have the *azaan*, call to prayer, said in her ear when she was born.

I was also very keen to be an active father. This was an alien concept in our community where men would have little to do with children especially if they were girls. A few months after our daughter's birth, Linda went back to work. It was unheard of in our family for women to work at all, let alone after they had given birth, whereas I saw things differently. Not only was I happy with my wife working, I did what I could to help. We saw parenting as a partnership. We shared the responsibility of taking and picking up our daughter when she was at the child minder who looked after her while both of us were at work. More generally, there was very little which had a particular gender label. The way I saw things, other than carrying a child in the stomach and breastfeeding, there was nothing a father could not do; cook, clean, iron. Whatever needed to be done, I would have a go without worrying whether it was a man's job or a woman's. Mind you, it helped to be living at a distance from my family and community. All these little things reinforced my being different.

A few years later, we had another child, a son this time. By then, I had begun to question whether I had any religious beliefs, even admit at times, at least to myself, that I had none. However, the cultural conditioning was too strong for me to say so to others.

I began to attend church with Linda and our children. This was made easier by the fact that the worship meetings were held in a hall instead of a church building. It would have been too much to actually walk into a Christian church; who knows who might see me?

There was a series of talks at the church on the topic of 'family.' By the time the series finished, I was used to going to the church. During one of my visits, one particular sermon spoke to me a great deal about the Christian faith. Its focus was on reconciliation. It reminded me of 'doing sorry' and also of the Tangerine Dream concert in the cathedral which was about forgiveness and reconciliation between Britain and Germany. The talk on this particular Sunday was about all the evils done by America against the native population. It was centred on a book by John Dawson, *Healing America's Wounds*. During the sermon the preacher also quoted the following:

> *O Lord, remember not only the men and women of goodwill, but also those of ill will . . . but do not only remember the suffering they have inflicted on us, remember the fruits we bought thanks to this suffering; our comradeship, our loyalty, our humanity, the courage, the generosity, the greatness of heart which has grown out of all this. And when they come to judgement, let all the fruits that we have borne be their forgiveness. Amen. Amen. Amen.*

(Words written on a scrap of paper near the corpse of a child in Ravensbruck concentration camp.)

I remember going up to the preacher and asking for a copy of the note and about the book.

In the book, John Dawson brings to America's attention the source of their pain—fear and prejudice. More critically, he helps them in practical ways to arrive at solutions for society and the church. He encourages his readers to see their history differently and to repent. He challenges them thus: "We *must* put the past behind us, but we must do it in a biblical way. Have we done that? Wounds that stand open and un-cleansed do not heal with the passage of time." Quoting Paul's letter to the Corinthians, he reminds us: "We have been given weapons that are mighty in God for pulling down strongholds but they are strange weapons. Among them: repentance, confession, forgiveness, reconciliation and restitution." The writer also points out that "We need to be in right order with one another." This was the third time I had heard about the concept of forgiveness in relation to the Christian faith.

This book also made me wonder whether there were wounds in Britain's past which needed healing. Who will pose such a question? Have I, after forty years in the country, earned the right to be critical of the nation which has given me a home and much more besides?

A little while later, I went to church on my own because my wife was not feeling well. This was a sign for me that I wasn't just attending to keep her company. In the middle of the worship service they began to sing the hymn, 'Faithful One'. This spoke of a God who was unchanging, who was ageless and who was a rock of peace that we could depend on. I began to wonder. Could he be my rock of peace? Could I depend on him too, in times of trouble and in the storms of my life? Maybe his love could be my anchor if I place my hope in him!

While the hymn was being sung, I became very emotional. I don't know what came over me. I looked up and caught the eye of one of the church elders. I walked towards him and suddenly started to cry on his shoulder. Although it wasn't clear to me at that time what this emotion was about, I had a sense later that it was me getting to know my real *Abba* Father (as in Aramaic, Abba in Urdu means daddy).

But one thing I had to have clear in my mind was that any decision I made towards Christianity would need to be mine. There had to be no possibility whatsoever that it was to please my wife or anyone else. I had to, with absolute certainty, own the decision and its consequences as mine.

Abba Father

It was a Friday evening, June 16 1995. As usual, I had just returned from the local gym. After my workout I had a habit of not showering at the gym but instead doing so at home. This meant that I could have a long soak in a hot bath, with a book, and stay as long as I wanted to or at least until my family called me out. But, this meant that after the workout I was very hot and sticky. After a few minutes in the car, the only thing I wanted to do was to get in that bath. I was not in the mood for conversation. Except on this evening things were not going to go according to my usual plans.

When I arrived home, a lady friend of my wife was there. I barely sat down when she said, "Khalad, I have a word for you." I had been in this situation with her once or twice before so I knew this meant a word from the Bible. She didn't wait for me to ask what it was; she began to read it:

Therefore this is what the LORD says:

> *"If you repent, I will restore you*
> *that you may serve me;*
> *if you utter worthy, not worthless, words,*
> *you will be my spokesman.*
> *Let this people turn to you,*
> *but you must not turn to them.*

I will make you a wall to this people,

> *a fortified wall of bronze;*
> *they will fight against you*
> *but will not overcome you,*
> *for I am with you*
> *to rescue and save you,"*
> *declares the LORD.*
> *"I will save you from the hands of the wicked*
> *and redeem you from the grasp of the cruel."*

(Jeremiah 15:19-21)

I missed the first few lines, but by the time she mentioned the word 'spokesman,' I was definitely listening. From there on it felt as if someone was reading a letter which had been written specifically for me. I was utterly convinced that the words had been written just for me in my situation. She got to the end. I thanked her and made a quick exit.

I got in the bath and settled down with my reading but could not concentrate on it. After a few minutes of reading but realising that it wasn't going in, I decided to put the book down. I then began to reflect on the Word I had been given. But this reflection was not just for a few minutes. It continued for the rest of the weekend. Quite a few times I read the Bible verses so I could understand them. But I did so when my wife was not looking. I didn't want to be seen showing interest in her faith and get her excited. Also, if I was going to move towards her faith then this was going to be my decision and mine alone. Nobody would be able to accuse me of making it under pressure or to say I had gotten carried away in the heat of the moment.

I was being told in no uncertain terms by God himself that I needed to repent and serve him and he would restore me.

I grew up in a world where what your neighbours said steered your life's course. Initially, many decisions I made were according to how others would see them but slowly this had changed. I had begun to do my own thing and had developed an attitude of not caring what my relatives and family would say. By now I had also become part of another set of neighbours.

During the past quarter of a century in England, I had surrounded myself with a certain type of person—liberal, political and usually godless. How would this world respond to what I was about to do? How would my friends in the Labour Party, in the anti-racist and equality movement and other such groupings respond when I told them about my beliefs?

But God was telling me not to look to others but let them look to me; I was to be his spokesman! I had to speak worthy words. I was not to follow others, instead I was to lead. What did that mean? Was my focus to be on my family, my community of origin, my current community or all of them? He did not specify. But, above all else, he was promising me that he would keep me safe.

But what did I have to do? Become a Christian?! When this thought first entered my head, I almost said it out loud: BECOME A CHRISTIAN! This had never been done in our family or community. But then neither had many other things which I had done before this moment. I went through the list in my head. No Pakistani had befriended the Sikh boy at our school, joined evening classes while still under 16, continued studying while working, bought a house when he didn't need it and without the support of his family. No one refused to get married in the way I did, taken an English wife after a wedding ceremony in a Christian chapel but not expected her to change her name or to wear Pakistani clothes. And, of course, there was my father before who had made plenty of his own decisions which were seen to go against the grain of our culture. There were plenty of times when I heard people in our family say, "What do you expect? You only have to look at his father!"

Throughout the weekend, my wife could not shut me up. I just wanted to talk. Sunday came. We went to church which was normal practice now for Sunday mornings. Throughout the rest of the day, I wanted to discuss Christianity, God, church activities, the Christian community . . . but I tried to do it without being seen too interested in it all. I obviously failed because by late evening my dear wife said, "I think you are ready to make the commitment." In response I said, "I think I am." There! It was said. There was no going back. There was no more pretending that I was not interested in Christianity. There was no more publicly saying one thing and privately thinking another.

We looked at each other so as to work out the next step. My wife said, "You can do it now." "What now, here?" I don't know what I was expecting, but I certainly didn't think that one could make a commitment to become a Christian in his living room with his wife. Perhaps I thought I would do it in the presence of some holy looking person wearing robes! "Yes, here, now", she said. I must say, when she said "You may want to bow down," it felt much better. After all, it was something holy, although I also appreciated the 'ordinariness' of what I was doing; no airs and graces in the presence of this God!

While I was bowing down, she said some words. I can't recall what she had said but it meant something at the time and I said "Amen." Afterwards, we hugged each other. It was a long hug, very emotional. I might have shed a tear. Afterwards, I phoned a few people to tell them what I had done.

I am quite a rational person. Having had my childhood world taken away, I relied on the structured and logic-based English world. It became my security blanket to replace the little, tattered *pernaa*, scarf I had as a child. The little understanding of religion I had at that time was to do with rules and requirements. But now here I was with another side of me being appealed to.

I didn't know the first thing about the Bible. I was at the point of following Christ purely on the basis of what I had seen in the behaviours and actions of his followers. I had read bits of the book of Job and used it with my pupils on one occasion as an example of poetry, but that was pretty much the extent of my knowledge of the Bible.

I had found myself in this place just once before, when I fell in love with my wife. That was also a 'heart' instead of 'head' decision. As for then, if someone had asked me now what I thought I was doing by becoming a Christian, I wouldn't have been able to give much of a response. Surely, as a Pakistani I should remain a Muslim; good, bad or indifferent.

It was definitely a new relationship I was entering into. For many in my world, this in itself was an alien concept. How can one have a relationship with God, the One who is meant to be worshipped, to be feared, to be addressed properly—according to a set script in a holy language one doesn't understand, and even then only after one has done proper ablutions and put on clean clothes?

Nevertheless, I was determined to go against the grain and make the biggest decision of my life.

The next day, on my way to work, I decided not to listen to any music during the 40-minute drive. I wanted to think about what had happened the evening before. What did this mean? I was a Christian. YOU ARE A CHRISTIAN! I said it out loud quite a few times.

Soon after, I decided that I did not wish to keep my news private; at least, my fellow believers should share in the decision. One day, everyone will hear about it. So I decided to be baptised.

I arranged to see one of the Pastors at my church who explained what baptism meant. He began by reminding me that God, my Father, has always known everything about me, as spelt out in Psalm 139. He summarised it for me and recommended I read it through on my own.

He then explained that baptism was a word in common usage among the Greek speaking peoples of the New Testament times. It had many everyday uses. For example, they 'baptised' fabric; it came out very obviously changed. They also 'baptised' tools and weapons in water after they were made very hot. This plunging changed the internal of the metal. The tool was now able to hold its cutting edge.

In the early church, baptisms were sometimes very public events while on other occasions only believers were present. Jesus himself was baptised by John in the Jordan. As he came out of the water, he saw heaven being torn open and the Spirit descending on him like a dove. And a voice came from heaven saying, "You are my Son, whom I love; with you I am well pleased."

He explained to me that baptism in itself does not save us from our sin. It also comes with a sacrifice. It asks of the new Christian, me, to stand out for Jesus, to stand up and be counted.

It was pointed out that those attending will watch the burial of someone they once knew and witness my resurrection to a new life by the grace of God.

The Message, a Bible translation in contemporary language, explains baptism like a migration where one leaves a country where sin is sovereign. We pack our bags and leave the house where we grew up. When we go under the water, we leave the old country of sin behind; when we come up out of the water, we enter into the new country of grace—a new life in a new land! Here, there are new and different ways of doing things. Clearly the challenge is to stop living like we are still in the old house in the old country.

It explains what baptism into the life of Jesus means. When we are lowered into the water, it is like the burial of Jesus; when we are raised up out of the water, it is like the resurrection of Jesus. Each of us is raised into a light-filled world by our Father so that we can see where we're going in our new grace-sovereign country.

So, our old way of life is nailed to the cross with Christ, a decisive end to that sin-miserable life. We are to be no longer at sin's every beck and call! Because we are included in Christ's sin-conquering death, we also get included in his life-saving resurrection. We know when Jesus died, he took sin down with him, but alive he brings God down to us.

Another way to see it is by comparing it to language. Sin speaks a dead language that should mean nothing to me but God speaks my mother tongue, not just Urdu but Pahari. As a born-again person I am called to be dead to sin and alive to God. I am called to be like Jesus as this is what he did.

The day came. If June 18 1995 was THE day, then this followed a very close second. Perhaps what had begun then in private was to be made public today. Sunday 9 July seemed to be dedicated just to me and our family. It felt as if there was nothing going on in the rest of the world.

All the hymns for the service had been chosen by me. This was a new kind of poetry, God's poetry, I had discovered. We began with *Lord I Lift Your Name on High* : 'Lord I love to sing Your praises, I'm so glad You're in my life, I'm so glad You came to save us.' We acknowledged that He had come from Heaven to earth to show the way and from the earth to the cross to pay our debts.

This was followed up with *Great is the Lord*: 'In whom we have the victory, who aids us against the enemy. We bow down on our knees.'

Early on in the church service, I was interviewed by the most senior church leader. He was a 'father' figure for everyone since he had founded the church. I had decided what I wanted to say and written some questions for him to ask me:

- What made you decide to become a Christian?

- Did anything happen recently which has been of particular significance?

- How does it feel having made the decision?

- What next?

There were a couple of things to note from my responses. I said that having *experienced* Christianity at the hands of its followers, I was now going to learn about its theory, starting with the Bible. "I am also going to try to change and challenge my own and other people's perceptions; to establish the fact that Christianity does not have a colour or a culture. Christianity is not limited to any race or group of people. No matter what your race, colour, nationality or language, God speaks to you."

The church, of which I am now a member, does not believe in child baptisms. It is left up to the child to be baptised when they are old enough to make their own decision. Instead, parents of newborn children give thanks in front of the church congregation and other family members who are invited for the occasion. Given that when our two children were born I was not a Christian, we did not have a thanksgiving ceremony for either of them, so we decided to do it on this day. A number of people who were significant to our family came up on stage to pray for us and our children and thank God for them. We also had the church pastor pray for God's blessing on our marriage.

We then sang another hymn, *I Believe in Jesus*. This was an opportunity to declare that He is the Son of God, who died and rose again, paying for our sins. We then acknowledged that he is here now, standing in our midst, with the power to heal now and the grace to forgive.

We then went to a nearby church for the baptism, given that our church did not have a baptism pool. A large group of our friends and family were already there.

We sang a few more hymns beginning with *I'm Accepted, I'm Forgiven*. We acknowledged being Fathered by the true and living God and being accepted without condemnation, guilt or fear. Instead, there is joy and peace as we release our worship to our Lord.

I was wearing old clothes so that I could step into the water fully clothed. Two dear friends, my brothers, stood on either side of me in the pool. One of them asked me if I accepted Christ as my Lord and Saviour and the answer from me was a definite and loud "YES!" They then said they were going to baptise me in the name of the Father, the Son and the

Holy Spirit. At this point, I was submerged into the pool and brought back out. I had died and was re-born. My old life was no more. My New Life had begun. I heard a mighty cheer from all who were gathered there.

I was led out of the pool and another dear friend, who I have also come to see as a brother, was standing there with a towel to wrap around me. Another couple of hymns concluded this gathering. *What a Hope I've Found.* He will never leave me; He is always there, waiting to be near me. Jesus, friend forever. More faithful than a mother. And finally, I was able to declare *I Will Give You Praise.* I will sing Your song, and bless Your holy name. For there is no other god who is like unto You. You're the only way. You are the Author of life. Only You can bring the blind their sight. Only You promised You'd never leave. Only You are God.

Afterwards, we had a party to celebrate, with cakes and drinks provided by friends and family. I received cards containing best wishes from many friends who were there and some who could not make it:

> *We were so delighted to hear that you had become a part of God's family, and our prayer for you is that you will know your God and make Him known. "The Lord bless you and keep you, the Lord make his face to shine upon you and be gracious to you. The Lord lift up his countenance upon you and give you peace" (Numbers 6:24-26)*

> *May God bless you abundantly on this special day. "You have made known to me the path of life; you will fill me with joy in your presence, with eternal pleasures at your right hand" (Psalm 16 verse 11)*

> *We rejoice with you today! Praise the Lord for his perfect work. We trust that the Lord will bind you together as a family and mightily bless you all. May he give you the desires of your hearts.*

> *We are so thrilled that you are walking every day with Jesus. It is an answer to our prayers for you, especially our daughter's. We pray that you will find fulfilment and challenge in your new life with Jesus*

> *This is the day that I have longed for, God has planned for, our friends have prayed for and you have been prepared for. I pray you enjoy it and are able to fully appreciate God's Blessing as you take this step in obedience. I pray you will continue to become the Man of God he made you to be. All my love*

Now I did not need any script for my prayers, or to be told when I should pray. I could do it anytime, anywhere, anyhow. I didn't need to do any ablutions before doing so. I could pray in English, in Urdu, or even in my Mirpuri dialect which would not be considered a proper language in most situations, certainly not when speaking to God or his Son. Who knows, one day we may even have the Bible in Mirpuri. It would have to be an audio recording since the dialect is not written down.

Now I did not need to work hard to get into heaven. I had all the entry qualifications I needed, since the One I had decided to follow was speaking on my behalf. He knew me so well that my name was written on his hand exactly as it should be, in its original form in Urdu; no need to worry about mispronunciation or misspelling.

Jesus had given his life so I could start with a clean slate, with all the filth washed away. As the hymn says, as far as the east is from the west, that's how far he has removed my transgressions from me.

I was now in a personal relationship with Christ. Although he is the King, I knew if he suddenly turned up I would call him by his first name and speak to him as one does to a mate, without any airs and graces. Who knows, we might even go out for a bite to eat and drink together!

I felt free! It was as if a load had been lifted from me. I no longer needed to pretend one thing and believe in another. Although being born-again can be a bit of a cliché, for me this was for real. Soon after I was baptised, I came to realise that the 'old me' did die that day and I was given a new life. I could now stop running away from God. Also, God was no longer the Judge I would face on the Day of Judgement but one who had come down to my world and given me a helping hand. My sins had been washed clean. So now, even if I was to face him, I would not be afraid to do so.

So I have become a Christian. I have given my testimony and been baptised in front of my fellow believers and a few others. We have sung hymns and eaten cakes. Is that it? Job done?

But I was reminded of Psalm 139, as the pastor told me about. Another reading of it reminded me that the job was not done but had only just begun. With the help of the psalmist, I was able to understand that the Lord has searched me and knows me. He knows when I sit and when I rise. He perceives my thoughts and is familiar with all my ways. Before a word is on my tongue, the Lord knows it completely.

I am told that I am fearfully and wonderfully made.

Slowly, it began to dawn on me that God, my Father, had been there in my life for a lot longer than I realised. I don't know whether He was there during my childhood but He was definitely there with open arms as my Abba, my earthly father let me go through the glass doors at Islamabad Airport. He was most definitely there helping me through my battle with my whole family during my first visit back when they were all pressurising me to get married. He had rescued me from I-don't-know-what in Pakistan because I discovered many years after leaving that my favourite teacher at secondary school liked to spend time with boys. God had been there in England to rescue me from all those risky situations during my life of adventure and exploration and will go on being there in the times yet to come. Many years later, I continue to realise that He has been there as a Comforter for my parents during all those early years and is there still with my mother.

Of course, it was He who brought Linda into my life and used her as His instrument to transform my life in the way only He knows.

Now, Jesus has become the brother I never had. And my Heavenly Father and the Holy Spirit have taken my earthly father's place. Only, unlike his, theirs is not an imaginary presence.

Jesus, my friend, my brother

So who was this Jesus whom I had decided to follow? Someone, somewhere was bound to ask so I had better have an answer ready.

In my earlier life in England when every question was explained with reference to my being a Muslim, I might have said that he was a prophet of God, one of the one hundred and twenty four thousand, according to the *Hadith*, Traditions. But now, I knew he was more than that. Yes, of course, he was the King of the universe but he was also a friend and a brother. If he was here now in person, I might text or email him to say, "Hey Bro, fancy going out for a drink? Maybe we can go for a balti too."

But who was he?

A long, long time ago, the prophet David spoke of him as the Rock. Later, the prophet Isaiah spoke about a Messiah who would suffer for the sins of all people. In those Old Testament times, it was difficult to believe that God would choose to save the world, not through a glorious king, but rather through a humble, suffering servant, whose strength would be shown by humility, suffering and mercy.

The prophet tells us that:

> *He would have no beauty or majesty to attract us to him, nothing in his appearance that we should desire him*

He would be despised and rejected by men and would take up our infirmities and carry our sorrows

He would be pierced for our transgressions and for our iniquities

His punishment would bring us peace and by his wounds we would be healed

He would be oppressed, afflicted and would be led like a lamb to the slaughter

(Isaiah 53:2-7)

I knew what this last bit meant. I had grown up learning about a prophet who was asked to sacrifice his son and that at the last minute God had rescued the son by sending a lamb to be sacrificed in his place. It was explained to me that this was the event we marked at the big *Eid,* festival. It is one thing to kill a lamb but it is something quite different to think of God's chosen servant as that Lamb who himself was sinless but would die for our sins. I certainly had plenty of sins which needed to be forgiven so that I could start again with a New Life.

What was prophesised many years before did happen. One day Jesus was out with his friends when God showed up, enveloping them in a bright cloud. A voice said to them, "This is my Son, whom I love; with him I am well pleased. Listen to him." But wasn't this the same man whose mother gave birth to him amongst the animals in a stable? I could just picture the scene. There were a number of poor families in our village when I was growing up who shared their sleeping space with their animals. This was definitely counter-cultural; a king being born in a stable! His humility was obvious.

Just before the Passover Festival, Jesus knew that the time had come for him to leave this world and go to the Father. The evening meal was in progress. Jesus got up from the meal, took off his outer clothing, and wrapped a towel around his waist. After that, he poured water into a basin and began to wash his disciples' feet, drying them with the towel that was wrapped around him.

As a child I learnt that touching someone's feet was the most humble act anyone could perform. I had seen situations where the bridegroom, just before leaving the in-laws' house with his bride, would touch the mother-in-law's feet as a sign of his humility. In a rural culture, like the one in which Jesus lived, people's feet are quite likely to be very dirty. This was radical indeed; a king touching and washing his followers' dirty feet.

Also obvious was Jesus' counter-cultural behaviour. For me, this was summed up in his teaching method where he starts "You have heard it said . . ." and then goes on to say " . . . but I tell you." He uses this approach to teach about dealing with anger, lust, divorce, vows, retaliation and how to respond to our enemies.

He called people from all walks of life to be his followers, including fishermen, political activists and 'despised' tax collectors. Looking at the bunch of people he chose as his followers gave me plenty of hope that there might be a role for a peasant like me. I had been referred to as a *jungly*, country bumpkin, by my mates and my father had the most menial of roles as a *chapraasi*, peon or office gofer.

Jesus associated with the poor and the despised. I had seen some of this modelled by my father. The way he treated the poor, the hungry and the low status people was very Jesus-like. I could understand its significance. When asked by an expert in law "Who is our neighbour?" Jesus responded by telling a story, which is found in Luke 10:30-37:

> *A man was going down from Jerusalem to Jericho, when he was attacked by robbers. They stripped him of his clothes, beat him and went away, leaving him half dead. A priest happened to be going down the same road, and when he saw the man, he passed by on the other side. So too, a Levite, when he came to the place and saw him, passed by on the other side. But a Samaritan, as he travelled, came where the man was; and when he saw him, he took pity on him. He went to him and bandaged his wounds, pouring on oil and wine. Then he put the man on his own donkey, brought him to an inn and took care of him. The next day he took out two denari and gave them to the innkeeper. 'Look after him,' he said, 'and when I return, I will reimburse you for any extra expense you may have.' (The priest and the Levite assistant to the priests were Jewish religious leaders, but the Samaritan was from a neighbouring foreign people group, despised by Jews)*
>
> *Jesus then proceeded to ask: "Which of these three do you think was a neighbour to the man who fell into the hands of robbers?" The expert in the law replied, "The one who had mercy on him." Jesus told him, "Go and do likewise."*

Ever since I came across this story, I have imagined my father being that Samaritan. He was the sort of person who would cross the road, not to avoid a needy person but to reach out to him. Mind you, the way Pakistanis are perceived in England and elsewhere, if Jesus was telling this story now, it would probably be called the Good Pakistani.

Jesus was everything; Son of Man, Bread of life, Light of the world, Gate for the sheep, Good shepherd, the vine. But he presented himself very humbly. The Bible says about him, "While being in very nature God, he did not consider equality with God something to be used to his own advantage. He made himself nothing by taking the very nature of a servant, being made in human likeness. And being found in appearance as a man, he humbled himself by becoming obedient to death— even death on a cross! But, God exalted Jesus to the highest place and gave him the name that is above every name, that at the name of Jesus every knee should bow, in heaven and on earth and under the earth, and every tongue acknowledge that Jesus Christ is Lord, to the glory of God the Father." (Philippians 2:6-11)

And then, Jesus made the biggest sacrifice he could have made for us; to die on the cross so we could be forgiven. And while he is breathing his last breaths, he asks his Father to forgive those who were responsible for his death, "for they know not what they are doing." No wonder he claimed to be "the way, the truth and the life". (John 14.6)

Reconciliation

Early on in my Christian life, I learnt about reconciliation through a letter from the apostle Paul to his friend Philemon. This was a letter of *sifaarish*. In the Pakistani context, if you are applying for something and you want your application to be treated favourably by the recipient, it would be to your advantage to get a letter of support, of *sifaarish*, from someone whose opinion counts in the eyes of the recipient and whose recommendation would, therefore, help to add weight to your application.

Paul was writing on behalf of Onesimus. It was a personal plea for a slave who had stolen from his master, Philemon, and then had run away to Rome where he met Paul. It was there that Onesimus had responded to the good news and had come to follow Christ. So Paul was writing to re-introduce Onesimus to Philemon, no longer as a slave but as a brother, and to ask him to accept and forgive him. Their past relationship and the additional barriers erected by the theft were to divide them no longer. They were to be one in Christ, brothers.

The notes in my Bible asked: "What barriers are in your home, neighbourhood and church?" In another place, it was explained that reconciliation means re-establishing relationships. Christ has reconciled us to God and to others. Many barriers come between people—race, social status, sex, personality differences—but Christ can break down these barriers. Jesus Christ changed Onesimus' relationship to Philemon from slave to brother. Christ can transform our most hopeless relationships into deep and loving friendships. That is what I wanted.

I prayed. With God's help I made a list of people with whom I needed to be reconciled and be forgiven and move into a different kind of relationship. I asked God to knock down the barriers that existed in our relationship.

My children had witnessed unacceptable behaviour from me, such as swearing, arguing and shouting. I prayed that it would not leave a mark in their lives and that I would be able to replace it for them with many more positive memories and experiences. I thanked the Lord for my dear wife and her resolve. In spite of the opposition from her own family, the cold reception from my parents and all the objectionable behaviour she endured from my relatives, she hung on in there, determined to be a loving wife and a caring daughter-in-law. For many years, she had to put up with the knowledge that my family expected me to take another wife, instead of her or in addition to her. After all, my father had two wives himself. I prayed that, in due course, she would find it in her heart to forgive all of us. Putting up with me during those 15 long years, I am sure was a challenge which only she could know.

I had realised that much of my wife's mistreatment was not so much personal but because she was a woman and a *white* woman at that. The culture I had come from had a very low opinion about them. Had I internalised such ideas? Whose forgiveness do I ask for and how? Maybe this was to be another area of *doing* forgiveness.

Then, there was my relationship with the wider world and the different people within it. While still in Pakistan, I had heard stories of paki-bashing. This was where white men would abuse Pakistanis and call them names. So, from an early age I saw white men as a threat, especially when they were young, in a group and had an aggressive look—the skinhead look. Now I needed to remind myself that such racists were the exception. I certainly could not go around assuming a white man was racist just because he looked a certain way. He could be as decent as the next man. He could even be a brother. I knew I also needed to forgive those white men and women who might have been responsible for racist behaviour towards me or who might have discriminated against me in the workplace or denied me opportunities in other situations just because I was a Pakistani. Using the last words of Jesus on the cross, I had to ask the Lord to forgive such people for they knew not what they were doing.

I had grown up in a community and a culture which had strong prejudices against black people. The term we used to describe them, *sheedi*, was expressive of this. Their one and only fault was their colour, given I was coming from a culture where being fair-skinned was considered beautiful. From my early days, I had formed some friendships with black people and had begun to conclude that beauty was more than someone's colour or looks. Mind you, coming to England at the time of the 'Black is Beautiful' movement had helped. Now, I was also discovering that many black people were my brothers and sisters. How should one respond to one's siblings? Not with a prejudiced attitude, for sure!

Then there were the nations associated with my Pakistani background. We began life as a nation hating Indians. They were the bad guys. They were the enemy. I remember our country's war with them in 1965. This was also when I saw some men in our village go and hide in the fields so they would not be sent to fight.

Although we knew there were many Muslims in India, we had an ambivalent attitude towards them. Why did they not come to the country which had been established for Muslims? As for other religions, we hated the Hindus and the Sikhs. I still recall the Sikh bogeyman my Mum used to tell me about as a child. But during my time in England I had begun to see the Indians as normal human beings. Still I knew I needed the Lord's help to take this many stages further. I added to my list my Indian friends. There were one or two who used to call me, and I them, *bhai*, brother.

There were the Jews. We had no direct link with them but because of the goings on in the Arab world and Palestine, as a Muslim I had learnt to develop hatred towards them.

Then there were Bangladeshis! They were the traitors. Why did they want to leave the country they had been made a part of in 1947? We had been told that they were helped by our historical enemies, the Indians.

Their war had happened at a crucial time for me, just after my arrival in the UK. More than anything, it made an impact on me. So I set out to investigate it. My eyes were opened. With the help of writers such as Syed Munawar Hasan and Aqeel Daanish in the pages of The Nation newspaper, Tahmima Anam in The Guardian and books such as GW Choudhury's *The Last Days of United Pakistan* I began to learn a new version of the history of a people who were once a part of Pakistan.

Apparently, right from the start, people of its eastern wing were treated as foreigners who, having lost one set of colonials, now had another set of imperialists, albeit from the same religion, who were controlling their life and liberty. While infrastructure was developed in the west the people of the east were neglected. As children we were never taught they were our fellow citizens. The Bengali people began to protest.

Soon after Partition, there had been a demonstration about language rights. They, quite reasonably, wanted their language to be given parity with Urdu. There was a shooting and a number of people lost their lives. They came to be known as the Language Martyrs. What was started then later culminated in East Pakistan becoming Bangladesh in 1971. It was given the final push by Zulfiqar Ali Bhutto. In the democratic elections which had just taken place, the Awami League and a few minor parties from the eastern wing of the country had won the majority of the seats—162 out of 300 in the National Assembly and 300 of the 600 seats in the Provincial Assembly. Having been in the west long enough I knew that the party which wins the most seats should form the new government. But not that year in Pakistan. There, Mr Bhutto, the leader of the Peoples Party, which got the most votes in West Pakistan, began to talk about *udher-tum-idher-hum*, "You there, us here." In other words, having won the majority of seats in the West, he wanted to form the next government; the east Pakistanis could do their own thing. Not surprisingly they did, with a little help from their Indian friends who took advantage of the situation and came to the aid of the Mukti Bahini guerrillas, who were fighting against the West-dominated Pakistani army.

Soon after, I volunteered my time to serve on the management committee of a local Bangladeshi and Pakistani community project, which was run by a Bangladeshi man. This was a practical response I could make.

I thank the Lord that the new country of Bangladesh, forty years on, has become a successful and thriving nation.

The Lord's work in me on reconciliation will need to continue for the rest of my life. I see this as a pre-condition to the bridge building role I believe I have been called to fulfil. With all of the above, I needed to be reconciled and be forgiven and move into a different kind of relationship.

In a strange way, I also need forgiveness from my own community. From very early on in England, I had realised that being a Pakistani was not very desirable. When I was called a 'paki' I had a tendency to point out that I was not actually from Pakistan but Kashmir. The writer Hanif Kureishi once said, that when he heard his white friends' parents talk "about race, about 'the Pakis", he was "desperately embarrassed and afraid of being identified with these loathed aliens". The word 'Pakistani' had been made into an insult for him. "It was a word I didn't want used about myself. I couldn't tolerate being myself".

My situation was not as bad as Kureishi's. However, when I was trying to establish myself as a mainstream professional, I did not always go out of my way to own my 'Pakistani-ness'.

At a personal level, when I come to think about situations like that described above, I try to remember the advice from the black American General Colin Powell that you don't have to see yourself as others see you. Of course, now I can remind myself of the words of my heavenly Father:

> *Khalad, you are fearfully and wonderfully made. You are lovely and I love you just as you are.*

Growing up

While sorting out my status as an immigrant, I was very aware that there was the emotional side of my experience which needed sorting too. The trauma of separation from my dear mother and father and my familiar world and being transported to an alien, albeit exciting, environment had left its mark on me. In my low moments, I felt as if I had been orphaned. As I grew up, I had a routine. If I wanted to get sympathy, usually from females, I would speak of my experience using a particular script. It often had the desired effect. It got me what I wanted. Although I was now a grown man, there were parts of me which were still that of a child. I decided it was time to deal with the past once and for all and move on as an adult. I should become the grown-up my children thought I was. So I decided to see a Christian counsellor. He had to be male. I did not any longer want to become a child and seek sympathy from a woman.

The counsellor followed a structured approach. He helped me to process how I saw myself in relation to my parents. Was I still their little boy or was I now a grown man who had become a dad? It was easy for me and for my parents when, each time I saw them, I stepped back into my *kurta-pyjama*, my 'little boy' suit. But this clearly could not go on forever.

During one visit to my birthplace, some twenty years after they had sent me away, it came to a head. My father kept going on about Linda. It felt as if the wider community was speaking through him and he was no longer the loving man who had welcomed her with open arms as if she was a daughter. Instead, he was now telling me I should have married a local girl, I should have married a Muslim, or at least should have made my *gori*, white wife, a Muslim and put her in *apney*, our clothes. I decided enough was enough. I began to respond. But this was not just a response to what he was saying at that moment but a response to the rubbish I had been getting from him and many others in the community over the years. It all came out.

I pointed out that I had married a wonderful, loving and loyal woman. I reminded him that since our finances were joint, half the money they would receive was hers. I said if it hadn't been for Linda, he and my mum wouldn't have gone to Mecca for their *hajj* pilgrimage. I also said that having been abandoned by them at a tender age and after many years in the wilderness I had been made whole because of this *gori*. I thought it was time I stopped pretending about my religion. So I said to him that my wife was more religious, more godly than I. This was too much to take for him. What had happened to his little boy?

All the time, my mother and young sisters were outside, scared out of their wits. They could not believe what they were hearing. No one had ever stood up to my father in this way. For me, this was another major turning point. Four years later, I was to listen to another Father.

The counsellor helped me to unpick my past life and process my experiences and the impact they had had on me. I had hardly any preparation before I was put on a plane to England and suddenly needed to grow up over night while missing my parents deeply. We explored how I had modelled myself on my father's independence and felt a strong sense of family loyalty and duty to support my parents.

The counsellor could see that I had a problem handling anger and conflict, with a tendency to bottle it up until there is a sudden blow-up. He saw that I had difficulty expressing negative or unpleasant emotions and that my dominant emotion was anger.

> *K finds it hard to come in touch with his own pain relating to his disappointments i.e. being sent to England, not having his parents around, not reaching his potential academically. At times, he feels guilty that he was not reaching the expectations of his family—both near and far away. His goals appear to revolve around affirmation from his loved ones.*

Spiritually, after a great deal of prodding, he was able to unpack that my *biggest hurt was my separation from my parents and being alone until my wife arrived.*

> *K felt worthwhile when he performed well at school and achieved his Master's degree and when he sent money to his parents. Now he also felt worthwhile when there were good wholesome family times. His experiences had led him to depend on his achievements and to seek affirmation (security and significance) from his nearest dependents.*

It was identified that I felt a particular sadness over being ostensibly abandoned over here and confusion as to how I should feel about it. I tended to make sense of it by thinking of the good things that had come from leaving Pakistan—but the loss had been hard to acknowledge.

It wasn't all negative. The counsellor noted that I had "a joy and trust which is refreshing." Furthermore, he noted that I had "a teachable spirit".

The counsellor helped me to see my real need to depend on the Lord for all my life's needs. The Holy Spirit had convicted me of my un-forgiveness towards my parents for the hurt I had experienced as a boy and for the trauma of changing continent, family and culture at such a tender age. The process enabled me to realise I needed to trust God's love and plan for my life and to involve Him in my marriage and my family relationships including those with my extended family. I was enabled to forgive my parents and start to depend on God.

The counsellor referred me to some Bible verses. Psalm 46 pointed out that God was my refuge and strength, an ever-present help in trouble. Therefore, I was not to fear "though the earth give way and the mountains fall into the heart of the sea, though its waters roar and foam and the mountains quake with their surging." It helped me to see that The LORD Almighty is with us; the God of Jacob is our fortress. At the end, we are told: "Be still, and know that I am God; I will be exalted among the nations, I will be exalted in the earth."

Then Romans 8 helped me to see who I had become. I was no longer controlled by the flesh but by the Spirit, "if indeed the Spirit of God lives in you. And if anyone does not have the Spirit of Christ, they do not belong to Christ. And if the Spirit of him who raised Jesus from the dead is living in you, he who raised Christ from the dead will also give life to your mortal bodies because of his Spirit who lives in you." This reminded me

that I could call God *Abba* Father and this had made me an heir—heir of
God and co-heir with Christ. But I had to share in his sufferings in order
to have a share in his glory. This was something to ponder on. I knew
in my birthplace an heir would inherit the land, the family home and
everything else that belonged to them and that with it came responsibility.
I had to work out what that responsibility was as a Christian.

Paul's letter to the Romans also reminded me that in all things God works
for the good of those who love him, "who have been called according to
his purpose." What was His purpose for me? The letter went on to point
out that since God "foreknew" me, I was "predestined to be conformed
to the image of his Son, that he might be the firstborn among many
brothers and sisters." I was called and justified and will be glorified.

The letter asks the big question: "What, then, shall we say in response
to these things? If God is for us, who can be against us? He who did
not spare his own Son, but gave him up for us all—how will he not
also, along with him, graciously give us all things?" Who will bring any
charge against me as one of God's chosen ones? I have Christ Jesus
who died—more than that, who was raised to life—sitting at God's right
hand speaking up for me and putting in a good word for me. As the
hymn writer has said:

> Lord, you are good and your grace is enough for me. Your power is made
> perfect in my weakness. When I struggle with sin, you still welcome me
> in. Even though my heart should be dressed in shame, it is Jesus you
> see, not the sinner in me.

He is the best *sifaarish*, reference, anyone could ask for. Who shall separate
me from the love of Christ? "Shall trouble or hardship or persecution or
famine or nakedness or danger or sword?" but, the letter then reminds
us of the perils such as persecution we might face. The notes in my Bible
point out:

> No matter what happens to us, no matter where we are, we can never
> be lost to his love. Suffering should not drive us away from God, but
> help us to identify with him further and allow his love to reach us and
> heal us.

I certainly needed some healing, I thought. The counsellor helped me
to set my wife and children free from having to approve of me, to see my
relationship with the Father as number one and to "develop a right and

humble self-image (not proud)". He encouraged me to "love without expecting praise/approval back."

This process has been a very important part of the restoration I was told about in those words of Jeremiah 15:19.

Jumping into others' shoes

After his death on the cross and resurrection, Jesus appeared to his disciples. He made clear to them the task that lay ahead. "All authority in heaven and on earth has been given to me. Therefore, go and make disciples of all nations, baptizing them in the name of the Father and of the Son and of the Holy Spirit, and teaching them to obey everything I have commanded you. And surely I am with you always, to the very end of the age." (Matthew 28:18-20)

I began to wonder what it might mean to make disciples in our modern world. One thing was quite clear to me: the task was not there just in relation to white people, or indeed to any particular race or people group, but to all nations. I began to reflect on the implications for our diverse society with its many cultures and ethnic groups. What did this mean in many of our towns and cities that are populated with people who have religion, no religion or who may even be anti-religion? We know that the diverse British people follow a variety of faiths other than Christianity. Some do so because they are personally committed to it while others follow a particular religion simply because they were born into it, and thus their culture dictates that they follow their community's religion. Above all, I began to wonder how, as a follower of Christ, I should carry out this task, known amongst Christians as the 'Great Commission', amongst my own Pakistani community.

I heard it said by preachers that we should lead by example. In the Gospel of John, it is said "If you hold to my teaching, you are really my disciples.

Then you will know the truth, and the truth will set you free." What does this mean, I wonder, to become disciples of Christ ourselves? Surely, as Christians, it requires us to understand Christ's teaching by studying the Bible and understanding its unique message.

Someone I know undertook a study of why Muslims convert to Christianity. He found that, "None of the respondents held the 'All religions are the same'. Or 'There is no difference between Islam and Christianity'. For them Christianity was unique." After all, Jesus said, in the gospel of John: "I am the way, the truth, and the life."

In my own study, I began to realise how radical and counter-cultural Christianity was. Here, the master washes the servants' feet; humility rather than force commands respect; strangers are welcomed, not just tolerated and peacemakers celebrated over warriors. I recall on one occasion our Queen said in one of her Christmas messages, "For at the heart of our faith stands the conviction that all people, irrespective of race, background or circumstances, can find lasting significance and purpose in the Gospel of Jesus Christ."

Early on in my Christian life, I discovered Lesslie Newbigin through an elder of the wider church who had taken me under his wing. Lesslie was from the UK and went on to become a bishop in India. Just before his death in 1998, he spent a few years in a multiracial church in England. In the book *Faith and Power,* he wrote that "We have allowed the Christian witness to be so domesticated within British culture that it has ceased to be heard as the radical message that it is." I believe it to be worse than that. Not only have others ceased to see Christianity as radical, perhaps we ourselves have come to see our own faith in the same way. Have we Christians allowed others to define Christ for us?

It is said, there is no persecution in the West. I would say that this may be so because we do not challenge the status quo, or 'how things are done around here'. We do not pose a threat to the world around us as it goes about its business. We go with the grain. What reason do people have to persecute us for we do not give them any!

I believe we live in times where, like the first disciples, we too are "sheep among wolves" and need to be "as shrewd as snakes and as innocent as doves." Like Jesus, we need to be confident, assertive and political. I recently came across a sermon on this subject through an internet search.

The Assertive Christian, by the Rev Dr. Harry Cahill of Babcock Presbyterian Church, begins with a dictionary definition of 'assertive': 'inclined to express oneself positively and boldly.' Then he asks us to look at the example of Jesus in order to understand what being bold and assertive means as a Christian. He wasn't rude, bossy, obnoxious or power-hungry, for these negative characteristics are the mark of an aggressive person. There is a difference. Being aggressive means being hostile and quarrelsome.

The speaker asks us to think of the many confrontations forced on Jesus in the gospels. We then realise that it was Jesus' adversaries who were the aggressive ones. It is worth remembering that people who act aggressively do so from a position of weakness. Jesus did not act from a position of weakness but out of strength and confidence. He did not lash out or get into a screaming match with anybody. He stood his ground.

Yes, I discovered he was humble and loving, spending his life giving himself away in the service of others. But he accomplished these things from a position of strength. How? By being the Son of God, Jesus had the perfect personality, fully integrated through his special intimate relationship with God the Father. Jesus was always in balance. But that doesn't mean Jesus never got angry at stupidity or injustice.

We only have to remember the time he drove the money changers out of the temple with a whip. Or look at the way he dealt with those in authority who abused the system for their own selfish ends, telling them "Woe to you, you hypocrites!" He was direct when he needed to be. For instance, when Jesus healed the man at the pool of Bethesda he was assertive. Jesus asked the man, "Do you want to get well?" prompting him to be assertive himself so he could participate in his own healing.

Jesus was also assertive in the way he dealt with people who wanted to follow him. In the story of the rich young ruler who asked, "What must I do to acquire eternal life?" Mark tells us, "Jesus looked straight at him with love and said, `Sell all you have, give the money to the poor, and then follow me.'" Jesus was honest and direct in using assertive love so that the young man could experience that same love.

In my view, the best example of Jesus' assertiveness is to be found in how he died. He was not a victim of circumstances. He didn't go to the cross kicking and screaming, begging for mercy. He allowed it to happen. On the day he was crucified, only Jesus was in complete control of himself and the situation around him. He demonstrated assertive love, when he said from the cross, "Father, forgive them, for they know not what they do." Yes, Christ was an assertive personality and, through him, I believe we too are empowered to be bold and positive in the way we treat each other and ourselves. Through Christ we are empowered to speak and live the truth in love and respond to the complex political situations we encounter in our diverse world where some wish to do away with Christianity.

As well as understanding our own radical faith, it is essential for us as Christians to understand those around us and their needs. Here I am talking particularly about my own Pakistani community. According to the elder statesman of the Christian world, John Stott, "the more we are aware of the people around us, the more urgent becomes our listening to God in order to hear a word from Him that is relevant to them and their pain."

We are called to 'love our neighbour as we love ourselves.' Who is our neighbour? How do we see him or her? Do we see the Pakistani community as a threat or an opportunity? If the former then we need to ask if that is Biblical. Is that how Jesus would see the community? I sometimes think that if Jesus turned up in our country, with his Middle Eastern clothes, language and habits, he might be seen as a similar threat.

On the other hand, if we see our Pakistani neighbours as an opportunity, then the challenge is to discover what is to be done to realise that opportunity as a part of God's purpose and plan, not just for us as Christians but also for the Pakistani community. Jesus died for me so that I could start with a clean slate—perhaps like a *takhti*, the kind I used to write on at primary school. I have no doubt that my name was graven on his hand in Urdu; no spelling mistakes there!

Pakistanis, like any other people, have multiple identities. I believe the worse thing we can do is to see their identity as that which is presented by the media or indeed that which they themselves sometime put forward when they are in the presence of Christians. They feel duty bound to say "We are Muslims" as if there is nothing else about them.

It goes without saying that the Pakistani community has a seriously bad press and needs all the friends, all the understanding and all the acceptance we offer. This is probably the last thing one would expect a convert like me to say. But I am simply doing what Christ teaches us. I would very much like to see the Pakistani community succeed, especially in the British context. I believe we have to find ways to get close to the community; to go beyond the superficial, to see the other, wider, aspects of their identities and to create an environment of trust so they are able to be honest and open with us.

When we are able to get close to the community, we then discover that they are men, women, old, young, married, single, divorced, students, restaurant workers, taxi-drivers or simply neighbours and fellow citizens.

We live in a complex world; therefore, our understanding has to be sophisticated. I believe Christians and especially those in leadership roles need to understand the basics of the Pakistani community and its religion and culture. I've lost count of how many of my Christian brothers and sisters think *Ramadan* ends in an 'm' or *imam*, religious leader, ends in an 'n' (*iman* means faith). Or the number who think that Mecca is a bingo hall.

It is only when we dig a bit deeper that we are able to distinguish a Sunni from a Shia, an Ahmedi from an Ismaili, a 'fundamentalist' (ah yes, that phrase coined, in the 20th century, by its supporters to describe a movement within the Protestant community of the United States) from those whose religion only has a cultural meaning. Then there are those who call themselves ex-Muslims, secular Muslims, progressive Muslims; the list goes on. I noticed that some Pakistanis felt confident enough in the security of the census form to declare they have 'no religion' as 600 pointed out in 2001 in one of the large British cities which has a large Pakistani community. This diversity is also an indication of the space we have created in the West so people can have religious freedom.

Growing up in a farming environment, I learnt that when it is time to harvest, if the labourers are not ready the crop goes to waste. With reference to Pakistani people being touched by the gospel and its outpourings, I have a sense that the Lord will go on withholding the harvest until the labourers are ready. The task is massive and competent labourers so few!

As part of my research for a project with a group of churches in the Midlands, I came across a mosque website where the local Muslim community had posted their *dua*, prayer, requests. Reading through them, one gets the impression that the Pakistani Muslim is just like you or me:

I took my GCSEs 2 months ago and the results are due in on Tuesday, please make dua for me that I do well and get the best grades to pass my exams.

(prayer for) protection from evil curse which has been blighting my life for years no peace at all in my life I feel so depressed and unhappy financial problems health problems please pray so that the curse be removed.

Please brothers and sisters make a dua that Allah gives us a baby. We have been trying for two years. Please Allah give us a baby. Ameen.

Please could you pray that I pass my driving test this Saturday inshallah, I have failed numerous times due to nerves and now I really need to pass so I can help my parents with daily errands, and not have to catch a bus.

Please pray to Allah that I and my mother may be cleaned and protected from black magic.

One of my points of connection with the Pakistani community in recent years has been as a parent. Imagine being the parents of one of the London bombers, the youngest who at the time was 17. On the day he and his friends carried out that most evil of acts, his parents were watching the 6 o'clock news. When they heard about the bomb, they looked at each other and realised it was their son the news reports were talking about. Whenever I am talking to a group of Christians about this, I ask them to put their hands up if they are parents. A few hands usually go up. I then ask them to keep their hands up if they know, at all times, where their teenage children are and if they know what exactly they might be doing. Most, if not all, hands go down at this point. Sometimes I also ask people to imagine how it felt for the parents of Irfan Raja.

Back in 2006, the parents of this 18-year-old schoolboy from Ilford became alarmed when he disappeared from home, leaving them a note in which he talked about going to heaven. He tried to comfort his parents: "Just in case you think I am going to do something in this country, you can rest easy that I am not. The conventional method of warfare is safer." His parents went straight to the police who were able to track Irfan and his four friends.

It is also important for Christians in the majority community to understand what it is like to be a minority who has settled in the British Isles, who came here to do jobs no one else wanted to do, at rates of pay no one else would tolerate. What are the current issues facing the community as a result of racism and Islamophobia? We know institutional racism at a general level but is there a version of it specifically affecting the Pakistani community?

What is it like for Pakistanis and Muslims? How does it feel to be like the Irish community of the 1970s, to be mistrusted and misjudged as a consequence of the behaviour of a minority from their community? In my view if Shakespeare was writing his plays today, the Shylock character would probably be a Muslim instead of a Jew; their community is our current 'Other.'

Then, there is language; a sensitive subject for people who have English as their first language, especially when it comes to learning third world languages. There is often an expectation in society that others should learn our language; no need for us to bother to learn Urdu, Pahari, Hindko, Pushto and so on. Monolingual Christians are no exception in this respect, but should be. We should learn from the experience of those who go to other countries. Many of them are experts in learning languages and cultures other than their own. Mind you, some inner city communities where Pakistanis live have a feel of another country.

I am reminded of the advice the character Atticus Finch offers to his daughter, Scout, in *To Kill a Mockingbird*. He said we never really understood a person until we considered things from his point of view; "until you climb into his skin and walk around in it". I wonder whether we Christians need to do a bit more of this when it comes to Pakistanis. Moreover, perhaps this should also include learning their language, as a tangible way to show them respect. Of course, you never know but you might get lucky and get an invitation to visit Pakistan or the city of Mirpur. They certainly don't speak English there.

Pakistani women, especially those born abroad, have particular needs. Because many of them do not speak English they need to be reached through their first language. Although official Islam gives many rights to women (according to one writer recently in the Muslim Weekly, Islam stopped the pagan practice of female infanticide, "granted rights of inheritance to women 12 centuries before they were granted to European women" and says women have to give consent for marriage), the lived reality for many Pakistani women is very different.

Until around the time I came to England, in 1970s, the Pakistani community here was comprised mainly of men. The community then began to bring wives over. Although probably half the Pakistani community is now made up of women, they are often absent in political and even social gatherings. For example, until recently, all the Pakistani elected politicians in local councils and Parliament were men.

From time to time, the wider world hears about women who challenge the orthodoxies of the community. Some 60% of marriages in the community are to first cousins, many of whom are brought over from Pakistan. Arranged marriages are the common way the community conducts its affairs in this respect; they are said to work better given the extended family system. However, the writer Ziauddin Sardar has pointed out that the boundary between arranged and forced marriage is sometime rather diffuse. What may begin as gentle persuasion can turn to unbearable persistence and end in outright force. The force itself can take different forms: a direct order from parents, a threat that the parties will be shunned by their families or the moral blackmail that the family will lose its honour. He points out that sometimes marriage is used to bring in nephews and nieces to Britain.

According to the Urdu newspaper, The Daily Jang, in 2008 there were over 3000 women victims of forced marriages in the UK. Many of these were Pakistani. Even here, a little more understanding would not go amiss. The writer Yasmin Alibhai-Brown, who writes for the Independent newspaper, once provided a helpful perspective on this:

> *This is a story which reveals the complexity, pain and confusion of migrant life. Last Friday Sekina Khan and Mohammed Bashir were jailed for the unlawful kidnapping of their daughter Rehana.*
>
> *She was a university-educated woman who refused a forced marriage and then (perhaps to punish her parents) went her own rebellious way, for a time even living with a drug dealer. They tried, but failed, to persuade her to change her mind. In the end they spiked her drink at a funeral and attempted to smuggle her away to Pakistan. She realised what was going on and raised the alarm. . . . .*

So do I believe that the parents jailed last week are monsters as the tabloid press would have us believe? Not at all.

Sakina and Mohammed are, by all accounts, decent folk who love their children. They have a corner shop in Bradford which makes relentless demands on their time and energy. Like many other immigrants, they thought this sacrifice was all that was needed to make a good life. They also believed that the children would appreciate this and not be seduced by the ways of the West and that they would all carry on happy ever after as if they had never left that spot in the sub-continent which is still home in their hearts.

Reading the above, I could picture my own parents in the same situation. Like this couple, they were loving but might have taken the law into their own hands given similar circumstances. Who knows! People do strange things when desperate.

As to younger women, they generally do better in education. However, according to Dr Tahir Abbas, an expert in sociology, they are expected to bear many of the family burdens, more than their brothers. This can include carrying out many of the family obligations, such as looking after relatives, even if this interferes with their studies which are seen as unimportant. Consequently, this can lead to the women dropping out of their courses.

Ziauddin Sardar has also pointed out that women are treated as cherished property and embody the family honour. Any offence they may bring to such honour can be very serious, given that being without honour and shame are among the most abusive terms: *bey—izzat*, without honour, *bey—sharm*, without shame.

There is also a problem with domestic violence, though from time to time men are victims too, especially those who have come from abroad. Just like their female counterparts, they may be unaware of their rights, lack competence in the English language and be financially dependent on the UK family. There is also the shame and stigma associated with being deported back to the village.

A recent report from a health organisation drew attention to the problem of infertility. Although this is not an issue only facing couples in the Pakistani community, they are perhaps least equipped to deal with it. Even when it is the man who is the cause, the blame is placed on the woman. Some women in the community also suffer at the hands of their in-laws if they fail to produce a son or have too many daughters. They often do not know who to turn to in such situations.

Then there are people on drugs with very few appropriate services and those who have found themselves on the wrong side of the law. It has been pointed out that nearly 13% of the prison population is Muslim, many of them Pakistani. Reading the report of one project in the Midlands, I realised that there is an alcohol problem in parts of the Pakistani community although alcohol is not allowed in the Islamic religion.

If there are members of the Pakistani community who are challenging its mores, who do they turn to? If they did turn to our Christian community would we know how to respond with a culturally appropriate welcome?

I am always reminded of the report about Bradford by the Pakistani trade unionist M Taj, *A 'Can do' City*, in which he noted:

> *It may be thought that the Christian Churches would have a limited role to play in a multi-ethnic area such as Manningham. On the contrary they have been committed and active in promoting good inter-communal relationships and in speaking out on behalf of the poor and disadvantaged.*

> *The Anglican Churches have shown particular vigour in this field and have maintained a considerable presence in the area, at a significant cost, with valuable effect. They deserve recognition from the wider community for their genuine goodwill and the positive effect of their efforts.*

I would like to think that Christian churches in other parts of the country would be similar in responding to the needs of the Pakistani and other minority communities.

Since 9/11, we in the West have become much more aware of the damage done by terrorism. Many people connected with it in a meaningful way for the first time.

For me personally, it felt as if the attacks had happened in my backyard. Throughout my adult life, I feel that I have had a close relationship with America and its culture. What had begun at school through the literature of Steinbeck and Lee was later reinforced through my interest in music, especially Bruce Springsteen, and TV programmes and films.

Perfect Storm is one such film. I have always been fascinated by small rural communities. The Massachusetts community of Gloucester where the film is set could be the village of my childhood. I can see myself in that community, trying to survive and being a part of the crew of that boat, the *Andrea Gail*. Probably the one character I see myself in the most was that of Bobby, played by Mark Wahlberg. Even his mum reminds me of my mum. And then there is Merv! It breaks my heart each time I see that scene when he is about to die and he says, "This will be hard on my boy."

Saving Private Ryan is significant film for me. Released in 1998, it is set during the invasion of Normandy in World War II. It follows Tom Hanks as Captain John H. Miller and his group of seven men as they search for a paratrooper named Ryan, played by Matt Damon. He is the last surviving brother of four servicemen.

I have seen the film so many times that all of the main characters seem as if they are my closest friends. There was so much in the film which connected with me. For example, the scene where the car arrives at Mrs Ryan's house, in rural America, to tell her that three of her sons have died, always makes me feel as if she could be my mother. Our village is up on a hill so you can see for miles if someone is coming towards the house. Watching the film helped me, for the first time after nearly 30 years of being in England, to connect with World War II. Many of those who had given their lives were volunteers. If it had not been for their sacrifice, there would be no Britain for me to come to and my father before that. I saw the film a few weeks before 11 November so that was the year I appreciated the meaning of the poppy.

Perhaps the two TV series which deserve a mention are *ER*, set in the emergency room of a hospital and *Homicide*, about the work of a police team. I feel as if the characters are my close friends. The other attraction in both the programmes for me is the positive portrayals for black characters. They could certainly teach British TV a thing or two.

I learnt about American government and politics as a part of my 'A' Level studies. During the 1990s, we as a family had the pleasure of visiting the country and gaining a firsthand look at many of the places which previously were just names on a page or in a song. We visited a number of locations including the centre of government in Washington and the historical foundations in Philadelphia, as well as exploring numerous aspects of the country in New York. The time we spent in our motor-home gave us the opportunity to see less well-known parts of the country.

So, on that afternoon when I saw the twin towers collapsing, it felt as if it was happening in my backyard. Later, I was helped to connect with what had happened by Springsteen. His album, *The Rising*, I believe has been one of the best responses to the events of that awful day.

In Britain, we were to experience something similar, albeit on a smaller scale, through the events of 7 July 2005. This was when four young men, three of whom were Pakistanis, carried out a suicide mission in London, killing many innocent people from across the world who just happened to be in London on that day. Many more were injured, some very seriously. I remember feeling such shame at being a Pakistani but then it began to strengthen my resolve to work even harder in promoting a more positive image of the community.

These two events have helped us in the West to have a more real understanding of what may seem to be just another news item.

On the day before the London incident, I travelled through London on my way to a meeting in the south of the country. I had come from Cambridge. There was a three hour hold up on the M25 motorway. It was later discovered that there was a little explosion in a white van which was carrying some sort of gas. Eventually, it was decided to get us off the motorway and redirect us through London. The next day, when news of the bombing came through the TV news, I remember thinking how lucky I had been.

I read a report which said that between 2009-2011 there had been 2488 suicide attacks in Pakistan leading to 3169 deaths and 9500 injured, many seriously. Each of these people mattered and had a right to life as much as any person in the West. Yet it is very easy to see this just as a set of statistics about a foreign place. We forget that each of these people had family, friends, plans and hopes, just like people we know.

In 2009, I remember feeling sick when the news came through that a bomb had gone off in Meena Bazaar, in Peshawar. Every major Pakistani city has one of these bazaars. It is where all the shops are which cater for women and families. These are the shops to go to for weddings. There were 137 people dead and 250 others injured. We were told that most of these were women shoppers. One young man of 17 had lost nine members of his family in the explosion. The family had gone to shop for a wedding ceremony. The victims included his father, mother, four sisters, brother, cousin and aunt.

Many shopkeepers lost their lives. In most cases, they were the sole providers for their families, in a world where few women work. Said Mohammad was one such shopkeeper. He was working at his small tea stall when the blast occurred, killing him instantly. He left behind his ailing wife Irshad and three daughters Bakht Meena, Bas Meena and Naureen. One of his daughters was quoted as saying that they expect hard times ahead, given the family does not have another male. "I have done my matriculation and have two younger sisters and a mother to care for. But, because of the social norms prevailing in our Pakhtun society, I cannot leave my house to do an office job," Meena said.

Most of the time, there appears to be a hierarchy about the value of life. In the book *Orientalism*, Edward Said quotes TE Lawrence, made famous by *Lawrence of Arabia*: "All the subject provinces of the Empire to me were not worth one dead English boy". Little appears to have changed since. Although we live in an age of information, it is rare to come across the personal and human stories of people who are affected by atrocities in places such as Pakistan. It becomes easy for us to look at them as mere numbers. We need to jump into others' shoes. We have to remember that each of those 12669 people, who lost their lives or were injured, were people like us.

There is a scene in the film *The American President* where the president gives an order to bomb a foreign country. He talks about how sorry he is, in that he had given an order that would lead to the deaths of many ordinary people going about their normal business. I wonder whether such reflection happens in real life.

You're Missing, a song from Springsteen's album The *Rising*, talks about a missing loved one who does not seem to be coming back. There are clothes hanging in the closet, shoes in the hall, a coffee cup on the counter, jackets on the chair . . . "Everything is everything, But you're missing." It really gets to me. It forces me to imagine losing a loved one in some bomb incident . . . .

Those 31 soldiers and cadets who were killed recently in Pakistan each had families who missed them. I wondered how many of their mothers and sisters were planning a wedding for them, but would now receive a dead body, if they were lucky. And the teenage suicide bomber; who was he? What was his story? Does anyone know; does anyone care?

Every time I read about those drones used to target the enemy, it makes me glad that my own birthplace is not a few inches north or west on the map. Otherwise, I would not see my mother and my childhood friends again. How many other Pakistanis and Afghans are there in the UK whose villages have been obliterated by such weapons and who will never see their families and friends again?

As the West mark another anniversary of that terrible day when planes struck the twin towers in New York, many in the Pakistani and the Afghan communities in the UK and elsewhere will quite rightly be wondering, "What about the deaths amongst our families and communities!"

This is just a snapshot of the Pakistani community based on my limited understanding. It's important to add to it. I urge fellow Christians to do some of their own learning. Many years ago I learnt about 'Action Learning,' a concept from Professor Reg Revans. This is an educational process whereby the participants study and learn from their own actions and experiences. It often does not require traditional instruction as it is done in conjunction with others as equals, in small groups called *action learning sets*. It enables people to reflect on and review their learning. John Stott similarly talks about people coming together to learn in a spirit of mutuality, like a book circle.

Being Christ

As well as understanding others at a deep level, we have to be Christ to others and do as he would have done.

The Bible asks us to emulate Jesus, so that when he appears we are like him. In Romans 12, we are given full details of what this means. We are called to offer our bodies as a living sacrifice, holy and pleasing to God and not to conform to the pattern of this world, but to be transformed by the renewing of our minds.

More than this, we are called to "be perfect, therefore, as your heavenly Father is perfect.". We are told to do as the Father does, so that we may be his children.

The modern workplace provides great opportunities for building relationships and sharing the gospel. It is one place where many adults spend most of their time and do so in a sustained way over a long period. For some of us Christians, this is the only place we are likely to encounter and have any meaningful contact with the Pakistani community. The congregation of one church I spoke at recently included business men and women, church workers, consultants, dentists, doctors, gardeners, home managers, lecturers, nurses, roofers, students, teachers, unpaid workers and youth workers. If each of these people did their jobs as if they were doing them for Christ or serving Christ as a customer or client, how much of a difference they could make! Is there a difference between a nurse and a nurse-who-is-Christ?

We are told that many in the Pakistani community still face unfair discrimination in the workplace because of their ethnic background or their religion or both. Is it possible that some of this is perpetrated by our Christian brothers and sisters?! If Christians are not perpetrators of some of this discrimination, they are quite likely to be witnesses to it. What should we do in such situations? Taking a stand against illegal practices would be a good start and would send a clear message to all concerned, especially to minority communities.

It is worth pointing out here that in the light of recent equality legislation there is now protection in the workplace against discrimination on grounds of religion or belief. Alongside rights, the law also brings with it responsibilities towards others. While this may present some restrictions in how we go about sharing our faith, it is well worth remembering that there is more to sharing the gospel than using words. From my early days as a Christian, I remember the advice proffered by St Francis of Assisi, to "preach the Gospel, use words if you have to." We would do well to remember this in many situations we encounter in our modern world.

In addition to paid work, many in our Christian community have hobbies. People in the above-mentioned church went walking, ate out in restaurants, went to the gym, spent time at the school gate, travelled in taxis, frequented their local chip shop, played football and cricket, read newspapers supplied by a newsagent, took their car to the garage for repairs or simply filled up at the petrol station. Any of these situations can be a rich source of opportunities for 'being Christ' to those around you. We should go about our normal business but be conscious of our relationship to Christ at all times. We need to be deliberate Christians.

In multi-cultural settings, this is bound to involve people of other faiths, many from Pakistan. What kind of impression do we as disciples of Christ leave on people who encounter us? Many Pakistanis are often hungry for contact and decent conversations with white people, including Christians. This is especially the case as the community in the UK suffers from social segregation more than any other ethnic group. Many in the community go through their life with contact limited to others from their own national origin. Sometimes, their world is restricted even further as they live amongst people who have all come from their particular region of Pakistan. In my Alpha course, I remember learning about Jesus being a bridge between us and the Father. Do we as His disciples have that role with the world around us? Many in the Pakistani community need us to build bridges between them and the mainstream white society or with other minority groups. Fulfilling such a role requires us to take the initiative in making contacts and developing relationships, rather than waiting for the right opportunity. If we are not careful, we could be waiting for a long time for that elusive 'right opportunity.'

There is a song by my favourite qawalli singer, Ustad Nusrat Fateh Ali Khan, called *tere wichon Rab disda,* I see God in you. Do people see God in us? Do people go away thinking: "I served Jesus today at the petrol station where I work?" Or "We had this group of white women who came to the restaurant I work at. There was something different about them. They were really well behaved, not drinking and shouting abuse at us. They were polite and considerate. They were also dressed modestly, not like some of their women you see. I think they were religious because before they started eating, one of them prayed and the others bowed their heads and said 'Amen'. If all our customers were like that then my work would not be so stressful."

I recently heard an excellent talk by the Christian speaker Nigel Hands on 'double listening'. In it he referred to the sociologist Grace Davie's research that tells us how people are more interested in 'belonging' than 'believing.' With reference to people of other faiths or no faith, before belonging comes 'watching' and 'observing'. We are being watched and observed all the time. What kind of message do we communicate through our words and actions? What will people take away after they have seen us or heard us? What kind of aroma do we, as ambassadors of Christ, leave behind for people who encounter us? It took me 25 years of such 'watching' before I walked into a church. It can be a slow process.

As a secret Muslim-background believer in Christ, there are times when my faith is a bit like the game *Taboo* where you are asked to describe something without using a list of words that are the most relevant to the topic. When I go and visit my family, in the UK or in Pakistan, I don't have any Christian literature with me. It would not be safe to use overt Christian language and yet I know I can share my faith with them. I am conscious that I may be the only bit of the Bible they are reading that day. More than anywhere, in such situations, I am conscious of being Christ's ambassador.

When sharing our faith, it is important for us to be aware of the distinction between culture and faith. We are all prisoners of our upbringing if we don't do something to break the chain and replace some of our conditioning with Biblical teaching. My past gave me prejudices towards white people (how they treat their animals better than their elders) white women (they sleep around a lot), black people, Indians, Bangladeshis; the list goes on.

I used to think being prejudiced was an issue for others. Then I realised that we Christians were not immune to this problem. What prejudices do we have as a result of our upbringing and cultural conditioning? Do we find ourselves in situations where what we say and do is more guided by our background, social class, education and politics than our faith? If so, we need to examine our behaviour in the light of God's word and start behaving as a Christian—in other words, do and say as Christ would do! Who knows what its impact may be. All the research done into the journeys of people who have converted to Christianity points out how essential that encounter with Christ-like Christians was.

I once heard a story on Unity FM, a Muslim radio station. It was told by someone at the Central Mosque of a white man who came to be converted to Islam. When asked why, he said "My neighbour speaks little English and has said only the occasional 'hello'. When I was ill in hospital he came to visit me each day. When I asked him why he said 'This is what our prophet has told us to do', so I became interested in this prophet and his religion, and here I am."

The philosopher Thomas Hobbes spoke of 'small morals,' meaning the small things in life. Many are so small that we are not even aware of them, until of course when things don't go as expected. On any given day, we are not likely to remember if the traffic stopped for us at a zebra crossing. We are not likely to recount the experience afterwards to our friends and family. But we would remember it if we spent a few minutes (just one would be long enough) and no one stopped for us when they could have. Each of these little incidents help to make life what it is. They make life different in one culture as opposed to another. They constitute the air we breathe in our lives. What contribution do we make as Christians in this respect?

One skill, I believe, we can all develop is to strike up conversations with strangers by asking really good questions and then to actively listen with interest to what they have to say. I don't mean the simple, throw away 'how are you?' when it's obvious that we are not really interested and we haven't the time to listen to their response.

Questions such as 'How is the family?' 'How is work?' What is your family's story?', when asked genuinely, can be real conversation starters.

During a sermon on the book of Proverbs recently, the preacher reminded us that "A cheerful look brings joy to the heart, and good news gives health to the bones." He spoke of a lady who had gone to the local Argos store and the shop assistant said to her, "Thank you for your smile. Whenever you come in, it makes my day." Is that all it takes to make someone's day? I was once waiting in the queue in my local fish and chip shop, which is run by young Pakistanis. The customer before me was a respectable-looking elderly white man. While he was being served he asked the shop assistant how he was. The young man smiled. Their interaction lasted no more than a couple of minutes but it showed they knew each other and will probably see each other in a similar situation. Maybe the man comes every Friday for his fish and chips.

We would also do well to remember that the Lord made us as relational beings, to be in relationship with him as well as with our fellow human beings. Relationships with believers are a key pre-condition in the journey to Christ for converts from a Muslim background; they probably are for most people. But this does not have to be a massive undertaking.

Life provides many opportunities for relationship-building. In many of our large cities, the taxi drivers are from the Pakistani community. They see some terrible sights and experience some awful behaviour at the hands of their passengers, especially on a Friday or Saturday night. I wonder, will they know the difference between Christians and the rest of the people they transport?

For a few years I have been going to a particular barber. It's about once a month and I am in his chair for about a half hour. It gives us an opportunity to catch up with whatever is going on in our lives. Sometimes, it's me who does the talking, at other times, him. There are no particular rules; it just happens. He is about fifteen years my junior. He is white and English. He knows about my faith journey and knows I don't swear so he doesn't use particular vocabulary he might use with other customers. We appear to have plenty in common with each other. We are both husbands, we both have mothers, he has two sons. When I told him about me having a good old cry when my daughter left for university, he said he couldn't imagine his children leaving home. His eldest is about to leave home for university. We both have working class origins. He is funny. I am serious. Not long ago, he said to me that he

saw me as a father figure. I looked at him and said, "But you are white!"
He knew I was joking.

What is the point of our relationship? I don't know where it may lead.
But, for now, it sure is fun when we meet. When I asked him to sponsor
me for a fundraising walk I was doing for a charity, he said he would go
one better. He offered to have my sponsorship form in his shop, and he
raised quite a bit of money. Much more important for me was knowing
that he valued my work and will have spoken about it to his customers to
persuade them to make a donation.

And then there is prayer. I don't know how many times the Bible tells
us to pray. We are told, "Don't babble on and on as people of other
religions do. They think their prayers are answered only by repeating
their words again and again." It is important to remember that our
prayer develops our relationship with God. Take any close relationship.
If we never speak to the person or listen to anything they have to say
then our relationship will quickly deteriorate. It is the same way with
God. Prayer—communicating with God—helps us grow closer and more
intimately connected with God.

If it had not been for prayer, I probably wouldn't be here today.
Unbeknown to me, there were friends and family praying for me during
all those years I was running away from God.

We are even called to pray for our enemies. Matthew tells us that, unlike
some religions that teach 'Love your neighbour and hate your enemy,'
we should love our enemies and pray for those who persecute us. Luke
spells it out even more: "But to you who are listening I say: Love your
enemies, do good to those who hate you, bless those who curse you,
pray for those who mistreat you." In my time in England, I have come
across a fair number of white people, including some Christians, who
instead of praying for Pakistani immigrants consider them to be enemy
'invaders.' This is especially the case in the past few years since events
like 9/11 were perpetrated by people in the name of religion. The fact
that even their own religious community do not consider them Muslims
has not entered the debate very much. Their actions have been assumed
to have been sanctioned by the whole Muslim community, who are then
punished through words and deeds.

After 7/7, it took me a while to process what had happened before I
could, with confidence, admit that I had come from the same country.

And yet, the Bible tells us to pray for them. Moreover, it is said "If your enemy is hungry, feed him; if he is thirsty, give him something to drink." What a radical faith we have!

For me, John Sentamu, the Archbishop of York, best sums up how Christians should respond to Pakistanis and Muslims: "I don't find any threat from a Muslim because I am a deeply committed Christian and my faith wants to treat them with dignity, love and care." But with a grin he adds, knowing it's not politically correct to say it, "Who knows, they may be converted in the process!"

Of course, we have to be able and willing to communicate our faith with others. It is particularly important to have an answer if we are asked a question or called to explain our faith. The Bible makes it clear: "Always be prepared to give an answer to everyone who asks you to give the reason for the hope that you have. But do this with gentleness and respect." (1 Peter 3:15)

In a situation where we are asked a question such as 'How can God have a Son?' it is important to be ready to explain that he was the Word of God in human form. When we look at Jesus, we can know what God's nature is like. Or if asked, 'If Jesus was the Son of God, why did his Father let him be killed?' one needs to be ready to point out the purpose of Jesus' coming as a kind of rescue mission to save people from the consequences of their sins. He certainly did that for me.

There is a white guy I have known for many years. I bump into him occasionally at the gym I go to. The other day, we decided to meet up and go for a walk in one of the parks nearby. He is bit of an expert when it comes to trees and plant life so he was giving me the lowdown on the green world which surrounded us. Just as we turned to start the return journey, he suddenly said: "So how did you become a Christian?" I wondered, after all the time we have known each other, why he wanted to know this now. I didn't ask but proceeded to answer his question. Since he had asked the question, I knew I had his permission to talk. I guessed we had about ten minutes before the end of our walk. I was able to share with him my journey to Christ and life with him since, explaining the transformation which had taken place in me. He would ask the occasional question but most of the time he just listened. I could see he was still interested in what I was saying as we parted company so it is possible that there will be a follow-up.

Here are some other questions one may be asked by a Muslim or someone with no religion:

- So what do Christians celebrate at Easter?

- Christians can sleep together before they get married, can't they?

- How can Jesus forgive sins today when you believe he died to forgive sins 2000 years ago?

- What do Christians really think of Muslims?

- How can Christians believe in the prophet Moses but not the prophet Mohammed?

- Doesn't the Bible teach Christian women to dress modestly?

If you are asked one of these questions, would you have an answer?

The Apostle Paul said, "Whatever you have learned or received or heard from me or seen in me—put into practice." (Philippians 4:9). Likewise, until we know Jesus well we will not fully understand the essence of his message that we are meant to put into practice.

Each week, a group of us email each other on a Sunday to share what is coming up for us in the week ahead so we can pray for each other in an informed way. Of course, things sometimes happen during the week which we have not predicted.

My recent email went something like:

> . . . This week I am visiting a few more schools to do pre-inspection inspections. I am also visiting Rochdale as a part of my consultancy work. The really interesting stuff is on Monday when I am attending the launch of a report at Parliament by a Cabinet member . . . .

If only I had known what the Lord had in his mind for me for this particular week!

As planned I travelled up and booked into a hotel north of Manchester. I had deliberately chosen this hotel because of its pool and sauna (I know it's a tough life!). After arriving and doing a few hours of work, I popped down to explore the facilities. I went on to dinner and more work before calling it a day.

The following morning, I nearly stayed in bed but thought I would work up an appetite for the cooked breakfast. So I went for a quick swim. Whenever I am travelling or am out and about in any situation, I try and strike up conversations with strange people in order to hear their stories. This morning was no different.

There were three people swimming up and down the pool with me. After a few minutes a bloke joined us in the lane next to me. A few minutes later we stopped at the same end, made eye contact, exchanged a few words and went back to our swim.

Later on I went into the steam room (I have to get my money's worth, I thought!). He was the only other person there. Normally, I start conversations but this time it was he who took the lead. He enquired what I did and then proceeded to tell me that he had retired on grounds of incapacity from his job, a lorry firm, and was in the army before that.

He said he suffered from being over-honest. Apparently, when he was given incapacity benefit he tried to return it on the grounds he did not deserve it because his firm had given him full pay. Realising this as a 'me too' moment, I felt this required me to contribute my own story. So I briefly told him my about the irregularities in my passport which had led me to return it to the government at a massive cost . . . .

By this time I realised I needed to have breakfast before heading off to work. I waited for him to stop talking. After a few minutes I realised the only way to stop him was for me to get up and look as if I needed to go. I then walked out but he followed me. "What do I have to do to get away?" I thought. Just then he said that he had been brought up in a religious home. "You know, as a Christian, but I don't have anything to do with such things."

When I asked why that was, he proceeded to tell me that when he was in the army he saw such terrible things and consequently turned away from God, wondering how he could allow such things to happen. I thought, now I have got to say something!

I said to him, "I am sorry, but I am in a hurry so I am going to be very direct." I then proceeded to tell him that I had converted to Christianity and that in some situations this could be extremely dangerous. I explained that the passport issue had come up after my conversion and my reading of James where it talks about sin of omission. I then said that while I couldn't tell him why God allows wars, he must accept that he was there all the time. Like the prodigal son in Jesus' story, he should come back home by finding a church. I left him with a promise that I would pray for him that he would find God and that we would meet in the next life. Will you please join me in praying that Peter from Greater Manchester comes back to the Father?

I guess the challenge for each of us is to be ready to tell our story or share what God has been doing in our life. This could be a conversation while travelling in a lift, in the changing room at the sports club, at the back of a taxi or some other situation; each one requiring a different length of conversation.

We also need to learn from the experiences and journeys of other believers. We all like quick fixes but we have to remember that it usually takes time. A person's coming to Christ is a team effort, like a chain with many links. For me there were lots of links over a 25-year period until the final link, which was coming to my church and being given those verses from Jeremiah. Like an assembly line, it is difficult to know what has been done before or what is to be done after. Although it's exciting to be the last link that causes someone to say, 'Yes, I want to follow Christ,' we are not called to only be that last link. What we are called to do is our little bit where we are to the best of our ability!

The Lord works incrementally—little challenges lead to bigger challenges. For me there was plenty of going against the grain before I arrived at this point on my journey. The bigger the decision one is making the longer it takes. There is no bigger decision than for a Muslim to convert to Christianity. So if they appear to be too hasty in wanting to follow Christ, they should be encouraged to consider such a decision very carefully with a lot of prayer.

Sometime people say one thing to your face, but privately they may be somewhere else. Right up to the last hours on my journey, my public statements were opposite of what I was thinking privately. Different ways for different people—people who come to know Christ have personalised plans.

To be one with God

I believe it is essential that whatever we do, we must stay close to God. My favourite passage for this is from Deuteronomy where we are advised "to love the LORD your God, to walk in obedience to him and to hold fast to him." This reminds me of my children when they were little, especially my son. He used to hold on to my hand when we were out and about in the world. If my hand became relaxed, he used to tell me to hold it tighter, in a vice-like grip. I imagine it made him feel safe. He was probably thinking, "My Dad is here, if I clasp onto him then nothing will go wrong." It is essential that, like my son, I also hold tightly to my *Abba* Father's hand as I take on the challenges of life. I may not be Gideon or David, but with God's help can I defeat the strong enemy I face daily.

A few years ago, we went to France for our family holiday. I am a laidback kind of person. On holiday, I often see people from the sidelines doing daring things like parasailing, being pulled behind a boat at a fast speed. Once or twice, I have wondered whether I should have a go. At least, it will give my children something to talk about. They are always saying, "All you do is read." We were staying in a static caravan near Lake Annecy. For a few days, I kept seeing these multi-coloured gliders appear from the side of a mountain, just as if they were wasps coming out from their nest in the side of a house. From a distance, it looked as if it was one person flying on his or her own. It was only when they got nearer that I realised that some of them had two people. I loved the fact they were going at a gentle speed as if they had all the time in the world; an antidote to our rushed and rushing world. It was a perfect scene.

I suddenly announced to my family that I wanted to have a go at gliding. They said nothing; I think it was the shock of me suggesting such a non-me type of activity. They did not try to persuade me not to do it. Linda did not raise the question of whether we were insured for the activity.

We made enquiries. There was a place we could go nearby. We phoned and made a booking.

On the day, I reported to the office and paid my money.

I was taken to the top of a mountain nearby. I was allotted my instructor. He showed me his glider and explained what we would be doing. All I had to do was get inside the tarpaulin 'sleeping bag' which was attached to his. So when he zipped us up, it looked as if we were one, two-headed, body. The sleeping bag was attached to the underneath of the glider. We stood on top of a slide.

The instructor explained, "We are going to run down the slide and you have to come with me; that's all. If you don't, then we are in trouble." I looked down the slide. There was nothing at the end of it. Just the tops of lots of trees. I tried not to be scared. I tried not to think about it. It was certainly too late to change my mind, given I had paid the money and my family was waiting at the bottom of the mountain looking out for my glider. So I said, "Okay!"

He said, "One, two, three." I remember the first two but not the third; I must have closed my eyes. When I opened them we were flying above the trees I had seen earlier.

I expected us to keep flying in a downward direction, towards the field at the base of the mountain, near the car park where my family was. But my companion had other plans.

He swooped down and then slowly jerked us upwardly until we were up above the place we had taken off from, so that he could wave to his friends and others who were waiting their turn for a glide.

We flew around for a few minutes. The instructor took pictures with the help of the camera he had attached to the end of the pole in front of us. He even managed to take a few seconds of video of both of us talking into the camera.

We went in and out of hot and then cold air. The instructor engaged me in conversation, which suited me because it meant I was not thinking about this brave (stupid!) activity I was participating in. After a while I went quiet. He asked me whether I had had enough. When I didn't answer, he realised I was feeling sick and took us down, though it might have been quite original to vomit while flying over the Alps. I was, however, glad when my feet touched the ground.

This experience illustrates my relationship with our heavenly Instructor. I had managed to do what was required by my gliding instructor, to be one with him and go down the slide-board before taking off. There are times when we have to be willing to go with our Heavenly Father on our own adventures. We have to *liptay raho*, keep on clinging to him. He also says, "Come with me and do as I do, so that to those who are watching we look as if we are one." Sometimes it is hard to follow him and trust him. I guess the challenge is to remind ourselves that, like the gliding instructor, He would keep us safe and use the process to develop us even further and let us have a bit of fun too.

When my son was little, one evening I was putting him to bed. As usual, I read him a story. He was lying on his bunk bed. I cannot remember what it was that we had just read, but it led me to ask him the question, "So, son, what am I good at?" He went quiet. He thought about it a bit more. I wondered what he was going to say. He then spoke. He said, "You are good at being Dad." This was very diplomatic given that I know I am not much good at most things except maybe a bit of reading and writing. After all these years of being a son, one thing is for certain: my Father is good at being my *Abba*, Dad. I just have to hold onto him and go into each assignment with him directing operations.

One of my favourite films is *Broadcast News*. It is a romantic comedy-drama film concerning a television news producer, a reporter and a news anchorman. The film helped me to realise that behind every anchorman there is a producer.

When my son was at primary school, I remember once we were talking about God being with us and he said "God lives in my head." I thought this was quite profound. Throughout most of my short Christian life, I have come to see God as my producer. I am the presenter but it is he who speaks instructions and ideas into me through the ear-piece. It is constantly switched on; I don't want to miss anything he may want to communicate. I go into situations with all sorts of important people and challenges. Without his ideas and direction, my work would be nothing. The film showed how the producer directs operations through an ear-piece. Every day, in my work and life generally, I go into situations where I would be lost without my ear-piece.

Many times, I have a vague idea of what I will say. But it is often impossible to predict what will come up or what will be said exactly. In such situations, I make sure that my ear-piece is in place. It may be invisible but it is definitely there. And the Producer never lets me down.

We are also advised in the letter to the Ephesians, "Be strong in the Lord and in his mighty power. Put on the full armour of God, so that you can take your stand against the devil's schemes. For our struggle is not against flesh and blood, but against the rulers, against the authorities, against the powers of this dark world and against the spiritual forces of evil in the heavenly realms. Therefore put on the full armour of God, so that when the day of evil comes, you may be able to stand your ground, and after you have done everything, to stand. Stand firm then, with the belt of truth buckled around your waist, with the breastplate of righteousness in place, and with your feet fitted with the readiness that comes from the gospel of peace. In addition to all this, take up the shield of faith, with which you can extinguish all the flaming arrows of the evil one. Take the helmet of salvation and the sword of the Spirit, which is the word of God." That, for me, says it all!

Prayer for my people

Throughout much of my time in England, I have been set apart from my family and community. My work, my leisure activities, the music I listened to and the books I read—let alone the fact that I listened to music and read books at all—all set me on a different journey from my fellow countrymen. Although I once was fluent in Urdu and even had written for the Urdu press, I was slowly losing my mother tongue. English had become my language. Occasionally, I would speak a few words in my dialect to relatives at some gathering but generally I moved in a world which spoke English. It would be fair to ask the question: was I Pakistani or was I British? In the world in which I existed most of the time, amongst decent liberal people, it was rare to be asked this question. So integrated had I become into the mainstream British world that I could just be me.

A few years after I became a Christian and got my new British passport, I went to see my parents. Many changes had taken place since I was last there, including the building of a rickety bridge at Dan Galli, over the River Jehlum. This meant that we could now take a more direct route to our village from Islamabad.

But because it had been a long time since I had been there, everything felt more foreign than usual. Having just travelled goodness knows how many hours and 'experienced' Pakistani customs, albeit better than before, I just wanted to be back in England.

We began our journey in the van-taxi my family had sent to pick me up from the airport. An hour or so after leaving Islamabad Airport, we turned left in or near a town called Dina and soon found ourselves stuck in a bazaar in a town called Choha Khalsa, named after the Sikh community that used to live there up until Partition in 1947.

I felt hot and bothered. I didn't want to be there. Instead, I wanted to be back home in my own world where I knew what was what. As we were waiting for the traffic to move so we could get out of this congested place, I said "Lord, why have you brought me to this place." Everything seemed worsened by the fact that I felt 'foreign.'

About that time, at our church we had begun to study Rick Warren's *A Purpose Driven Life*. I had barely finished asking my question when the Lord answered by quoting a part of the book to me. He made it clear that he had chosen for me to have come from Pakistan, from my village in Tehsil Dadyal, District Mirpur, Azad Kashmir. He had chosen for me to have the parents I have; to speak the language I speak; to make the religious journey I had made . . . the list went on. It shut me up. Early on in my Christian life, I had become reconciled with a long list of people. Now, the time had come for me to add my country of birth to that list. During the week-long stay I reflected on what all this meant. I now realised that the Pakistani people were also a part of God's creation and when Jesus died on the cross, he died for them too so their sins could be forgiven.

What was God's purpose in my birth to these parents, in this place and with this language?

For some time now, I have been aware that our God is a god of pre-condition; he creates the conditions, sometimes a long time before, so things can happen as planned. This, I believe, is what happened to me in relation to Urdu. Having gone away from my culture and community over many years, my Urdu deteriorated to such an extent that I could barely string two words together. English had become my natural language. So dominant was it that, if it is possible to have a second mother tongue, English is it for me. But the Lord had other ideas. Instead of learning French so I could communicate during our annual holidays with the people across the English Channel, I felt God was saying I should work on my Urdu. I felt a bit like Noah must have felt when, many years before the flood, he was asked to start work on the Ark. He must have felt foolish building a boat, given they had never had rain and there was no sign of it ever coming. People seeing him working on his project must have gone away convinced of his madness. It was the same for me.

Had someone asked me why I was learning Urdu instead of doing something useful, I would not have been able to answer them. But I carried on. That was how I came to be a regular reader of The Nation, then a daily but later a weekly paper published in London. Now each week, slavishly, I read my copy. I look forward to it being delivered on a Friday. The paper mainly focuses on news about Pakistan and Kashmir. Occasionally, it has news of my countrymen in the UK. About two thirds of the paper is in Urdu and the rest in English. In the early days, I would start with the English section and then just manage to read a few bits in the Urdu section. The English section at the back of the paper was definitely my 'front page' and the Urdu section the 'back page'. Now, it is exactly the opposite.

Reading the paper each week, including the sections which are quite useless to me such as the *rishta,* marriage partner, pages has made such a difference. I have started to use my weekly reading of the paper as example with my students when I need to tell them that 'practice makes perfect.' As well as getting stories, perspectives and comments I would not otherwise have, I have become much more confident in the Urdu language—even more confident than most of my fellow countrymen, in England as well as back in my birthplace, given that theirs is not a reading culture. Like Noah, I have come to see the point of what God had prompted me to do. There have been so many times in my 'Christian' work as well as elsewhere (isn't it all God's?) when proficiency in Urdu has been very useful, almost essential.

As a small child, *Pahari* was my mother tongue. When I started school, I was told the only language that mattered was Urdu. Neither of these nor other languages I studied in school, such as Farsi and Arabic, mattered when I came to England. "I might as well forget the other languages," I thought. They had no worth. Now, after forty or so years, I have come to feel that my English is perhaps good enough so I can afford to focus on my mother tongues. And, given it is the centenary year for the Pakistani poet, the People's Poet, Faiz Ahmed Faiz, perhaps I will now be able to read some of his brilliant works. People like him make one proud to be a Pakistani.

Just as my English Bible was becoming familiar and losing some of its excitement of the early days when I was first given it, I can now read the same passages in Urdu. Now I think Christ died for Pakistanis as well. There are even bits in my Urdu Bible which are an improvement on my English one. I remember I was so excited when I first found myself praying for my daily *roti* instead of bread. Recently, when reading Deutronomy, I felt *liptay raho* said it much better than 'hold fast'. Recently, I have started to read Song of Songs. In Urdu, it is called *Ghazal al-Ghazlaat*, which in English would be 'Ode of Odes.'

The *ghazal* is a poetic form originating in 6th century Arabic verse. In its style and content it is a genre which is used to express themes of love and separation. As well as in Urdu, the *ghazal* is found in many of the other languages of the Indian sub-continent.

Perhaps more significant than my competence in the language, I have a better understanding of Pakistanis and Kashmiris in England and in Pakistan. I feel the Lord has taken me back to the level of knowledge I had of the community in the 1970s; maybe better. He wants me to be the person he made me to be—an immigrant Pakistani who is now a British citizen, fully integrated into the mainstream society, who started life as a Muslim but is now a follower of Christ. He wants me to be me, not someone else. He has plenty of other people but only one 'me.' He has a purpose for me which is different from the purpose he has for others.

So Lord, thank you! Thank you for my birthplace and heritage. Thank you for my parents and the foundations they were able to lay for my life. Thank you for their decision to send me away to a foreign place, which was to become my home, where I could flourish and become the man I was meant to be according to your plans. Please, help me to step into my parents' shoes so that I have a better understanding of their sacrifice in sending me away. You Lord, as a father who sent your son to our world as a lamb to be sacrificed on the cross, would know what it must have been like for my parents to let me go, at such a tender age, away from them, to a foreign land.

During my early years, I had learnt enough about who I was and the world around me to have some notion of what the future would look like. Every time I listen to *The River* by Bruce Springsteen, I imagine my own similar trajectory as his character, with a local flavour. I imagine coming from down in the valley where when you're young, they bring you up to do like your daddy before you.

Even though it's a world where I would have had an arranged marriage, I imagined meeting my Mary in the high school and we'd ride out of the valley down to where the fields were green. We'd go down to the river and into the river we'd dive. Then I would get Mary pregnant and would have to get married to her in a hurry (actually, if this happened in real life, I would probably get into serious trouble but you can do anything in dreams!). Later, I also imagined getting a job working construction for the Johnstown Company and then losing the job.

I knew I would probably go as far as high school in Dadyal and then, or maybe while I was at college in Mirpur, I would get married. My *shaadi* would be a big affair. Everyone in the area would have an invitation. The *nai*, barber, would have his work cut out. He would not just pass the usual message to a few people he came across. Instead, he would have to stand in the centre of quite a few villages and shout out an open invitation to everyone to come and share in the celebrations. All the relatives who lived further afield would come and stay for days, eating and talking and whatever else people do at these gatherings.

I would have children, many children, especially sons. I would take over the household from my parents, looking after them in their old age. I would then grow old and slowly hand things over to my sons who would take over the household from me and on and on things would go, following their natural course.

Our house would continue to be a place where the hungry and thirsty are fed and cared for. Throughout my life, I would be surrounded by my friends, many of them would be boys of my age who would similarly become men and have their own families. The cycle of life would go on.

But no! The future was suddenly given a very different shape when my parents decided to send me away, uprooting me from my natural habitat and sending me to a foreign land, to go live next door to the white man and lead a very different life to the one I had imagined so far.

All these years, I have lived my real life as it has become and, in my mind, I have lived a parallel existence. I have lived the life I would have lived had I not been uprooted. I suddenly realised that, like the natural world, we humans also have an ecology. And mine was well and truly upset. And then I suddenly remembered the Lord saying, "If you repent, I will restore you." I have played my part in a small way and he has fulfilled his promise, many times over. It's not just been a restoration to the original but something far superior. Thank you, Lord.

It got me thinking about the ecology of a people, a community, my community. What harm has been done to their natural existence! What was the outcome when lots of the able men left to go to England, not just for a few days but many, many years? They left their parents, the girls they fancied and who they would have married one day, the wives and children, their land, their natural world, their familiar habitat. Later, they would bring their sons out of their community too.

And in their new world, they would have to fend for themselves; cooking and cleaning, things they always thought would be done by their mothers, sisters and wives. They would be in a foreign land where they speak strangely, write backward, eat *haram*, forbidden foods, drink what looks like urine. Here they would work hard, doing jobs no one wanted to do, work long hours and still be abused by the locals. What was all this doing to the ecology of these people? What restoration did they need? Who would restore them? If they repented, would the Lord say: "I will"?

The following cuttings from the Urdu weekly, The Nation, published from London, make clear the situation of the Pakistani community:

> *We are seen as terrorists or as harbouring terrorists* (1 April 2011)

> *Our younger generation in the Pakistani community faces many problems. They underachieve in education and then go onto use and deal in drugs, causing many to go to prison* (22 April 2011)

Many of the community's young people are at times wrongly targeted by the police and suspected of terrorism. Are the Pakistanis the new Irish who had had a similar experience at the hands of the police during the 1970s?

With some exceptions, the Pakistani community has not benefited to the same extent as others have from the opportunities available in Britain. The community continues to be divided according to *biraderi*, extended family networks. Its women continue to be discriminated against and excluded. From time to time community leaders make speeches and plead with the community to sort itself out but to little avail.

Lord, I thank you for the UK, its history, its institutions and all it has to offer. I thank you for the Pakistani presence here and ask that you help restore the ecology of the community, both here in the UK and in places such as Mirpur and in other parts of Kashmir and Pakistan.

At school in Mirpur, I had learnt about Tariq Ibn Ziyad, the man after whom Gibraltar is named. I now wish my countrymen would follow his example a little more. As the huge army of King Roderick was assembled before them, Tariq displayed the qualities of leadership that carried Islam to the far corners of the world.

In one of the most beautiful, eloquent and inspiring speeches in history, Tariq appealed to his men to stand firm, to remember Allah, and to fight till Allah granted victory, or death. But he did not merely offer empty words. Like the very best of leaders, he led from the front. He chose to lead the cavalry charge right into the middle of the mighty Spanish army.

When he asked his men, who would be prepared to follow him, every single soldier rallied behind him, choosing victory or death. In a brilliant psychological move, Tariq then ordered that his men to burn their boats. Today the English language has been enriched by this phrase, to 'burn your boats.' It means you are so determined to carry on that you have permanently closed the option of turning back. This dramatic gesture had three benefits. It convinced his men that they had no means of escape; it focussed their minds more sharply on the battle as they had everything to lose and everything to gain; it sent shudders of panic through the ranks of the Spanish army. What madmen were these, to burn their boats when they were so heavily outnumbered?

I pray that the Pakistanis in England, and wherever else in the world they have settled, would follow Tariq's example and accept their new country as their home, their own country and are accepted as such by those around them. The community can then begin:

- to thrive here by accessing the opportunities offered to them

- to play their full role as loyal and law-abiding citizens of the country

- to be good neighbours to those around them

- to rely on principles of merit instead of nepotism, *quome* and *biraderi*-ism

Aqeel Daanish once wrote an article, in The Nation, titled *dil heh Pakistan mein* (the heart is in Pakistan). In it he talked about how Pakistanis live in Britain as if they were still in Pakistan. He quoted advice from the then Prime Minister of Azad Kashmir, where most of the Pakistanis come from, as "Kashmiri and Pakistani people settled in Britain should behave as full citizens of this country" (meaning Britain). I say 'Amen' to that.

Lord, I thank you for our democracy and thank you for each and every Pakistani councillor, Member of Parliament, European Parliament, Scottish Parliament, Welsh Assembly and House of Lords and members of any other elected or properly constituted public bodies. I pray that they are able to serve the Pakistani community as well as their wider constituency and to help build bridges between communities.

I give special thanks for the contribution of the Pakistani women, as community leaders, councillors, Members of Parliament and in many other walks of life and pray that they come to provide role models for others and to help realise the potential of their community.

Dear God, I thank you for the religious freedoms we all enjoy in our country. Those of us who are from the Pakistani community are well aware that such freedoms would not be available to those of other religions in our country of origin. I thank you Lord that in Britain we can achieve according to our potential. No one ever asks us which family or *quome*, caste, we come from. I know that some who would be considered low, almost untouchable in Pakistan, have reached high positions in England. I also thank you for people such as Lord Ahmed and Lord Qurban who often try to bring this fact to the attention of the community. Lord, I pray that, in turn, the Pakistani community in England would allow the same liberties and opportunities to members of their own community. I especially pray for freedom for those who wish to change their religion.

God bless Pakistan and Kashmir

Pakistan continues to be a semi-failed nation. When it faces disasters such as the recent floods, people are disinclined to offer it charity, partially because of a fear that the money will line the pockets of the politicians as is often the case.

Sarawat Iqbal in one of his recent contributions in his aptly named column in The Nation 'I speak the truth,' said:

> It is complete lawlessness across the country. The courts have become political parties. No one is respected. The public is left no one to turn to; no one is interested in their concerns.

> Whoever can, is looting the nation. The honest officers are only those who have not yet had an opportunity to do so.

The minorities in the country continue to be persecuted. Those who speak up for them are treated similarly as was shown by the murder, by his own bodyguard, of Salmaan Taseer, Governor of Punjab, who was a liberal described by his son, Aatish Taseer, as a "cultural Muslim." His crime was to speak up for the rights of a Christian woman accused of blasphemy. Later the same fate was to befall the Minister for Minorities, Shahbaz Bhatti, who appeared to have been killed for his Christian faith and his views on the rights of minorities. As I write this, Mukhtaran Mai, who was gang-raped nine years ago, is still fighting for justice.

Raja Anwar wrote recently (22 April 2011):

> *At the creation of Pakistan, its founding fathers had imagined a nation where each and every one of its citizens would have economic and social protection. There would be no one crawling or begging on the streets of the country. The state would offer protection to widows, orphans and the unemployed. The society would be free from injustice and dishonesty. Corruption would not be the normal practice of politicians and leaders. No one would be able to steal or sabotage democracy or change government at the point of a gun. The nation of Pakistan would be a safe haven for minorities where everyone would be free to worship according to their beliefs and live a life of freedom*

The article sums up the many speeches of the founder of Pakistan, Muhammed Ali Jinnah. In his presidential address to the Constituent Assembly of Pakistan on August 11, 1947, he also spoke against nepotism. He asked his fellow Pakistanis to work in co-operation with each other, "forgetting the past, burying the hatchet." He said people should work together regardless of the community they belong to or their caste or creed and do so simply because they are citizens of Pakistan. In the same speech he made clear:

> *You are free; you are free to go to your temples, you are free to go to your mosques or to any other place of worship in this State of Pakistan. You may belong to any religion or caste or creed that has nothing to do with the business of the State.*

> *We are starting in the days where there is no discrimination, no distinction between one community and another, no discrimination between one caste or creed and another. We are starting with this fundamental principle that we are all citizens and equal citizens of one State.*

Recently, there has been press coverage about the activities of anti-corruption activist, Anna Hazare, in India. What has fascinated me has been the direct reference, by Pakistani commentators, to his work and a wish that a Pakistani equivalent existed. Arshad Mahmood wrote The Nation: "In Pakistan state sponsored corruption is the biggest challenge. It's a shame we don't have an Anna Hazare who can mobilise our citizens." I am glad to see that, unlike in the past, Pakistanis are now quite happy to want to openly emulate India.

My prayer for Pakistan is to see the sentiments of Mr Jinnah's speech become a reality; that the country becomes a sovereign, self-respecting and confident nation at peace with itself within its borders and in relation to its neighbours; that its politicians and bureaucrats become more focussed on servant-leadership rather than leaders who abuse and neglect the ordinary people of Pakistan and who line their pockets at the expense of the citizens; that the media and judiciary become free and responsible and that the country is able to make the best use of its resources, natural and human, in order to become a successful and developed nation. The writer Aatish Taseer has talked about a 'Pakistani ethos.' I pray that the nation finds an inclusive ethos, one which defines it positively and without reference to external enemies, imagined or otherwise.

Lord, I pray that the country would use its aid funding and international loans wisely and for their intended purposes, that its citizens, especially the very rich, would 'give to Caesar what is Caesar's' by paying their taxes and, in time, the country would spend more of its gross domestic product, perhaps the 5% recommended by the Organisation for Economic Co-operation and Development, on education and less on its armed forces and instruments of war.

Furthermore, I pray for the establishment of some sort of 'United Nations of Asia' so that there is peace and prosperity within the Indian sub-continent. And for a world free of war and mistrust, based on reconciliation and forgiveness with free movement across borders so people can become good neighbours. Europe can offer a model in this respect.

I seem to have an attraction for war graves and memorials. I became aware of this during our American trip many years ago. We visited the Vietnam Veterans Memorial. It was a very moving experience, very spiritual. Although I did not know any of the people whose names were listed there, it felt as if I knew them all. I wondered whether enough had been learnt from the loss of such lives.

More recently, during a holiday in France we visited one of the Second World War cemeteries. I was particularly moved to see graves belonging to the German soldiers who had lost lives in the same war. This was an area where the Germans were the enemy, and so to see their graves given the same space and respect as the Allied soldiers was very powerful indeed. Not a single one of them had been vandalised. Coming from the world I do, I could not imagine Indian and Pakistani or Pakistani and Bangladeshi soldiers' graves together and treated respectfully in such a way. And yet the question is obvious. Why not? If the British can sit at the same table with the Germans, then surely India, Pakistan, Bangladesh, Sri Lanka and Kashmir can all live together. Surely, there can be forgiveness and reconciliation between India and Pakistan and Pakistan and Bangladesh! After all, until 1947, we had a common heritage and our deeper foundations are the same. So, my prayer is for Pakistan to have good relations, based on principles of trust and co-operation, with all other countries which surround it, and especially for the people of India, Pakistan and Bangladesh to set their own agenda of love, peace and friendship across their borders.

Last but not least, I pray for my own birthplace, Kashmir. The UN Resolution of 13 August 1948 stated:

> *The Government of India and the Government of Pakistan reaffirm their wish that the future status of the State of Jammu and Kashmir shall be determined in accordance with the will of the people and to that end, upon acceptance of the Truce Agreement both Governments agree to enter into consultations with the Commission to determine fair and equitable conditions whereby such free expression will be assured.*

I pray that in the spirit of the above resolution, Kashmiri people would be given the opportunity to decide what they want through a free and fair referendum across all parts of this divided and disputed nation and that there would be communication and co-operation between Kashmiris across borders. Lord, you say, "Blessed are the peacemakers;" I ask that you bless the peacemakers involved in bridge-building amongst the Kashmiris.

As I write this, Mangla Dam is being extended. It will affect even more people than it did the first time. I pray for justice for the people affected, that they would be able to start life elsewhere.

The area I come from is wholly dependent on English money. Young people still grow up with aspirations to come to England as husbands and wives and benefit from government handouts rather than the opportunities here. Lord, I pray that this dependence would stop and that the community would become self-sufficient and develop their national capacity in other ways.

I ask this in the precious name of your dear Son, Jesus Christ.

Ameen!

Note

Just after I finished writing this, the front page headline in the Urdu section of my weekly paper, was a plea from Pakistan's Chief Justice Iftikhar: "things are not good. Please pray for Pakistan." While, on the inside back page of the English section, Dr Maleeha Lodhi, who had served as Pakistan's High Commissioner in London, was quoted as saying: "Pakistan needs a narrative of hope."

Then a few days later, one of my favourite columnists, Faz Zia, started her weekly column thus, "Today, every Pakistani's prayer is that our country is peaceful and thrives as a nation." Amen to that.

I *was an illegal immigrant!*

I realised that the decision had been made and declared in front of witnesses. Now I had to live it. So the task was not so much accomplished but had only just begun. Having made the momentous decision to follow Christ I had to answer the question: so what?

I had not read the Bible at all. I don't think using a part of the book of Job with my students at school counts. I made my decision simply on the basis of what I observed in Christ's followers, how they conducted themselves generally and towards me and my family. Other than the little teaching I had experienced at the church I had attended for a few months with my family, I knew very little about the Bible. If someone in my network of white friends asked me why I had done a crazy thing like decide to follow Christ I would need to provide an answer. While I had no intention of telling my own family and community of my decision—many of whom probably thought I had already joined the 'other side,' given the fact I had not made my wife a Muslim—I thought there may come a time when I would need to explain this odd decision I had taken. So, I decided that I had better learn about this new faith, at least its theory—I knew its practice from the Christians I had encountered.

After asking for advice from the church leaders and fellow Christians, I enrolled on the Alpha course. The publicity for the course said: "The Alpha course is open to everyone interested in discovering what Christianity is about. Come, relax, eat, share your thoughts and explore the meaning of life." So I cleared my diary for about seven or eight evenings. The first evening began informally, with a meal. There were about a dozen of us there. Quite a few were still unsure about Christianity while I had already made my mind up.

The course leader pointed out that Christianity had an image problem. It was seen as boring, square and only for weak people. Was Christianity true? Was it a blind faith?

The first session was titled 'Who is Jesus?'. The speaker set out to answer questions about Jesus' existence and his fully human nature—his body, his emotions, his experiences. We were asked to reflect on whether he was more than just a man, more than a great human/religious teacher. The session focussed on what Jesus had said about himself, all the "I am" statements he made, which are recorded in the Bible. We were given Bible references that provide evidence about Jesus' existence—his teaching such as the Sermon on the Mount, his works, his character, the fact that he was the fulfilment of the prophecy in the Old Testament and finally his conquest of death with reference to the evidence for his Resurrection.

We were given a course handbook which had two quotes from the writer CS Lewis:

> A man who was merely a man and said the sort of things Jesus said wouldn't be a great moral teacher, he'd either be a lunatic—on a level with a man who says he's a poached egg—or else he'd be the devil of hell. You must make your choice. Either this man was and is the Son of God, or else a madman or something worse. But don't let us come up with any patronising nonsense about this being a great human teacher. He hasn't left that open to us. He didn't intend to.

> Now it seems to be obvious that he was neither a lunatic nor a fiend; and consequently, however strange or terrifying or unlikely it may seem, I have to accept the view that he was and is God. God has landed on this enemy-occupied world in human form.

More than what was being said about Jesus and Christianity, the course was particularly significant for me because we could question things. Coming from my background, it was a refreshing change for me to be openly discussing such things and with the encouragement of a Christian church leader who was leading our course.

In the second session we explored the question of Jesus' death. He died on the cross not because he deserved it, but because he did it for us. By his death I am 'justified'—just as if I'd never sinned. We were told about the society Jesus lived in, where, if you could not pay your debts, you sold yourself into slavery. I could relate to this. I had heard about the many in Pakistan who for generations are 'owned' by their masters. Many of the people who work in the country's *pathaa*, kilns, fall into this category. Did the bricks for the house I grew up in come from the hands of such people?

So you are about to be sold into a lifetime of slavery and Jesus shows up and says, "I'll give my life so his debt is paid." Wow!

In the session we were told that Christianity was not about rules but about relationship with God. Religion or good works were not going to bring us close to God; it's what Jesus had done that was the key.

In a later session, we explored this further. In my notebook it says:

> *Just as with people with whom we have real and meaningful relationships, we don't only talk at a particular time and place and in special words, then we shouldn't do so with God.*

It was explained that:

> *The Christian life is a process of becoming more and more like Christ. This process will not complete until we see Christ face-to-face. But, knowing that it is our ultimate destiny should motivate us to purify ourselves.*

It was explained that 'to purify' meant to keep morally straight; to keep free from corruption of sin. I certainly needed to purify myself and keep away from sin.

The course leader pointed out that we all have areas where temptation is strong and habits are hard to conquer. These weaknesses give the devil a foothold so we must deal with these areas. I had a few habits and ways of thinking I had to deal with and where I needed God's help. Time will tell how successful I am at doing so.

We were told that "all Scripture is God-breathed and is useful for teaching, rebuking, correcting and training in righteousness, so that the servant of God may be thoroughly equipped for every good work." More than anything, the Bible is a love letter from God to us; it tells us how much God loves us.

There was a session titled 'Why and How do I pray?' It was explained that the whole Trinity was involved in this process: to the Father, through the Son and in the Spirit. I learnt that prayer was two-way; we talk to God and he talks to us. Why would God want to talk to little me! Later, my notes say:

> *Praying in a special place, at a special time, in a foreign language I don't understand is not what it's about then!*

The session answered questions such as:

- Does God always answer prayer?—ask and it will be given to you

- How do we pray?—just talk in your own words

- When should we pray?—When two or three are gathered in my name there am I with you; God is always with you, everywhere.

We had a number of sessions on the Holy Spirit—who is he? What does he do? How can I be filled with the Holy Spirit? These were big questions which needed time to address. Later on, we also had sessions on subjects such as how to resist evil and how we should tell others about our faith. Here, we were told that the Bible asks us to "go and make disciples of all nations." Did the word "all" include my family, my community too! Soon after, I did tell a few members of my close family that I had become a Christian. I also advised them to behave as if I hadn't told them.

At the end of the course we were given a statement which we could make as our Prayer of Commitment:

> *Lord Jesus Christ*
>
> *I am sorry for the things I have done wrong in my life (take a few moments to ask His forgiveness for anything particular that is on your conscience).*
>
> *Please forgive me. I now turn from everything which I know is wrong.*

Thank you that You died on the Cross for me.

Thank You that You now offer me the gift of forgiveness and eternal life. I now take that gift.

I ask You to come into my life by Your Holy Spirit to be with me forever.

Thank you Lord Jesus.

As I had already made my decision to follow Christ, all there was left for me to say was "Amen."

When the course finished, there were still many questions I needed to explore. Coming from the background I had—Muslim followed by secular—there was much more I needed to learn. Soon, I was to sign up to a theology course with a consortium of Christian colleges. I was disciplined enough to study 150 hours every six months in order to complete a Unit. I did an assessment of my week to find out what time I had and how I was spending it. I concluded that, out of my 168 hours each week, after allowing for time for my work, leisure and family I still had many hours left. I did not watch TV on at least two evenings a week. With that and some other time I had been able to find, I was able to finish the course. I could have carried on for another three years in order to achieve a diploma and a further three years to achieve a full degree but I decided that for now a certificate was enough. I had got enough of a grounding in my new faith to help me answer a tricky question or two which might be thrown at me. But in many ways, this was a matter of lifelong learning.

While I was going through the Alpha course, we as a family also decided that we would pay a tithe to the church so it can meet its financial commitments. Although the New Testament does not specify an amount or percentage, the teaching in the Old Testament talks about giving 10% of one's income to the church. So this is the amount we settled on.

For an immigrant who had gone through the hardships I had, to actually voluntarily give away my own income was a major decision. It was also a major step to give my money to a white organisation. I don't think my family would have understood but then they wouldn't have understood the decision I had just taken which lay at the heart of tithing. So their opinion did not come into it. In some ways, it was quite an easy decision to take. In my mind, following Christ and following his teaching went hand in hand.

We filled in a form that was sent off to our bank to give them permission to take a regular amount each month from our joint account and transfer it to the church's bank account.

But then something really amazing happened. Within a few weeks of tithing, completely by chance, while going through some papers, I realised that my employer had made a mistake in the amount I was being paid each month. I asked the personnel department of the employer to investigate. They did so and, as a result, I was given back-dated pay which was more than six months worth of the tithe we had just agreed to pay. For me, this was a clear sign that the Lord was saying, "My son, I recognise the step you and your family have taken. Here is a little amount to get you started." More than that, he has continued to bless us with generous provision ever since and we have every confidence that this will continue.

I also noticed a change of heart in me in that I was much more willing to share my property and belongings with others. In the past I was much more possessive of what was mine but now it was as if I had come to see it all as God's, for me to give back to him or share with fellow Christians. Once I recall coming back home in the middle of the day, unannounced. When I came through the front door, I realised there were quite a few people in the house with their children running in and out of different rooms. In the past this sort of situation would have freaked me out. I would have thought, "How dare they be here in my house when I did not know about it or agree to it?" But now, I thought "Oh well, don't mind me, friends, and carry on as before. What is mine is yours to share."

The church we belonged to was mainly white. At the time this was what I needed. I needed a bunch of white people to welcome me amongst them, to accept me unconditionally and treat me as their own. This they did and did so genuinely. Looking back over the years, they have become my family, my extended family and community. They would be the first people I would turn to in my hour of need and joy (with some exceptions, allowing for the white British reserve).

For my part, right from the start, I became integrated into the life of the church. Unlike some, I did not develop a consumer attitude towards church, where you expect that you can sit back and let others meet your needs. I began to serve in a range of roles: children's church, men's ministry, driving the minibus or general pastoring. At the same time, I grew in my faith, sometimes in the company of more mature believers. At the worship services, coming from a non-singing culture, I would often mime the hymns, reading the words and learning from them. Some of the hymns became my personal prayers. The church I belonged to sang quite a few songs by Graham Kendrick. *Shine, Jesus Shine* became a favourite.

Another hymn that came to be a prayer for me was *Be Thou My Vision*. I have included it here in full:

> *Be thou my vision, O Lord of my heart,*
> *be all else but naught to me, save that thou art;*
> *be thou my best thought in the day and the night,*
> *both waking and sleeping, thy presence my light.*
>
> *Be thou my wisdom, be thou my true word,*
> *be thou ever with me, and I with thee Lord;*
> *be thou my great Father, and I thy true son;*
> *be thou in me dwelling, and I with thee one.*
>
> *Be thou my breastplate, my sword for the fight;*
> *be thou my whole armour, be thou my true might;*
> *be thou my soul's shelter, be thou my strong tower:*
> *O raise thou me heavenward, great Power of my power.*
>
> *Riches I heed not, nor man's empty praise:*
> *be thou mine inheritance now and always;*
> *be thou and thou only the first in my heart;*
> *O Sovereign of heaven, my treasure thou art.*
>
> *High King of heaven, thou heaven's bright sun,*
> *O grant me its joys after victory is won;*
> *great Heart of my own heart, whatever befall,*
> *still be thou my vision, O Ruler of all.*

I was very happy to belong to this community of loving people but I was conscious that I needed to meet others like me who were followers of Christ. At times, I felt that no one had ever decided to do what I had done. So I decided to investigate whether there were other Asians, Muslims, Pakistanis or Kashmiris who had taken the same step out of their faith and converted.

My search led me to an interesting and diverse group of people. There were Indian Christians, Pakistani Christians; Sikhs and Hindus who had left their gods and were now following *the* Way, *the* Truth, and *the* Life. I came across white Christians whose life was wholly devoted to sharing the gospel through word and deed. Later, I was to meet people, who, like me, had converted to Christianity. Amongst them there were one or two from my own Mirpuri community. I also enjoyed meeting my first Bangladeshi brother. This was a special moment given the history of our two countries.

As a reader of books and literature generally, I found a range of Christian literature, including some in Urdu. Later, I was to be a part of fellow Christians' efforts to translate the Bible into Mirpuri/Pahari dialect. Who would have thought that the humble words which came out of my community's mouths were proper enough to use for the Word of God. What affirmation!

All these Christians managed to become a part of my wider reference point. There would be times in my life when I would turn to them for prayer, for encouragement and sometimes just to be in their company as brothers and sisters. This was while I continued to become integrated into my own church—it was slowly becoming more multi-racial—and become a part of its leadership serving in a range of roles. There is always plenty to do. For me, church is both about giving and receiving, often simultaneously.

During this time, I read books by people such as Steven Masood and Gulshan Esther, both Pakistani Christians. Later, I was to meet them both. I remember thinking how strange that they looked normal, just like any other Pakistani and yet they were Christian. Maybe, one day there will be many more of us. They obviously belonged to a time when converts had to change their name to something which sounded English and western, just like my community's desire that women like my wife should change their names. I am glad to say that no one has ever suggested to me that I should change my name. We know that my Father is happy with Urdu; he has no trouble pronouncing or spelling my name. In fact, I often see my name graven in Urdu on Jesus' hand as he breathed his last breath on the cross. I know it was my sin that killed him.

Given my enthusiasm for my new faith, I began to tell the occasional friend about it. I remember telling a friend about the tithe. Like me, he was a self-made professional from a respectable but not wealthy family.

When I told him, the look on his face said it all: 'What, give your own money away!' I did tell him that God had paid me back for most of it but I don't think he believed me.

Soon after, I invited a colleague to a Christian meeting. My note said something like, "in my Father's house, there are many rooms and there is a room set aside for you." He thanked me for my letter and then told me how, having been brought up a Christian, he had gone away from it. He said he saw no evidence to believe in God and saw religion as being incompatible with reason or rather, the best and most informed reasoning.

I didn't know what to say. Here was an intellectual response to what I saw as a matter of the heart. I had fallen in love. How do you put that into words?

A couple of years later, this colleague said to me, "Why is it you never talk to me about your faith?" I said it was because of his letter. He then said that I should feel free to talk about Christianity anytime I wanted to. It made me wonder whether, like me, he also had a public and private position when it came to such matters of faith.

One day, a few years after becoming a Christian, I came across these verses from James 4:17: "Anyone, then, who knows the good he ought to do and doesn't do it, sins." This got me thinking about various aspects of my life. But above all, it made me think about how I had been sent to England under a false identity.

Over the years I had looked into the details of this matter and fully understood what had happened. But growing up in a culture where it was a case of 'if you can get away with, it's okay to do it,' I thought nothing of it. I was also part of a community where I was not the only person who had been sent to England this way. More generally, there was an acceptance of telling lies to get through immigration, social security or anything else to do with white people or their institutions. But now, surely, as a Christian, every time I used my passport identity, I was telling a lie. Since I knew the identity I had been given was false, by not telling the authorities I was committing a sin.

Such 'passport identities' were commonplace in our community. There were a number of my friends at school and elsewhere who had similarly been given a new identity. The details of this were explained by Yaqub

Nizami, in his book *Pakistan sey Inglistan tak* (from Pakistan to England), published in 2006:

> *Pakistani immigrants in the UK were good at taking advantage of the system. They discovered that being married was more tax efficient; even better if you had children. So when they went back to their villages to see their families, they would return claiming they had got married and had a child, usually a son; some would claim they had twins. (Of course, it was easy to provide documentary evidence; anything is possible for a little bribe!) Later, when people began to bring wives and children to join them in England, they could bring the son(s) of relatives who fitted the age. It didn't have to be a perfect match; give or take a few years.*

So this happened to me. In fact, if it hadn't, I would still be in Pakistan leading a different life. I was given the identity of a child who did not exist and his *dateofbirth* which I later discovered meant date of birth. This was when I was supposed to have been born. I did look into my real birth date. It turned out I was born a couple of years before my passport date of birth.

Linda and I discussed the whole issue with the church leadership. This was no small matter. We had to act wisely. We prayed. We researched the matter by speaking to people who were experts on immigration. I recall phoning one of the government's own immigration advice agencies. They said I should do nothing. "You don't have to. If you really want to revert to your true identity, just change your name by deed poll." I knew this involved going in front of a lawyer and making a statement. I thought this advice was clearly according to the world's ways. And I was trying to follow God's ways. So I decided to ignore their advice. We thought some more. We then decided to act. This was to be my reconciliation with the British society and its systems. How does one ask for forgiveness from a nation? Maybe it was to be my 'doing sorry' that I had learnt about all those years ago!

Having decided to go ahead with our decision to disclose the whole matter to the government, we hired the services of a lawyer. Upon his advice, I began to gather testimonials from a number of people who had known me over the quarter of a century of my life in England. A letter was then prepared by me and sent, through the lawyer, to the government:

Our client has come forward of his own will without any legal necessity to disclose information about his true identity. The reason for doing this now after many years of being in the country and using the false identity is to do with his conversion to Christianity.

As a result of the teachings in his church he has embraced and recognised the importance of values such as truth, honesty and integrity. Such is his belief in these values he feels it is important that the authorities are informed of his true identity. Indeed, it would have been easier to leave matters as they stand as our client was under no legal requirement or need to disclose. The matter of his identity could also have been resolved by a simple change of name by Deed Poll.

It is his belief and integrity which has resolved for him to declare all the facts.

We believe the documentary evidence submitted here will without a doubt confirm that he is committed to life in this country with his family.

The above was followed by four pages of information about my full background, how I came to be in England, my achievements here, employment, education, family life and commitment to the wider society as evidenced by the extensive unpaid work I had done. It was pointed out that I was a model citizen who had not once claimed social security.

The immigration authorities took about one year before they informed me that they were not going to deport me. What do you mean, 'deport me'?! I had come forward when I didn't need so that I could live a life based on truth. I had been in the country over twenty five years. I was at home. Where would they have deported me to? However, they took my British nationality away. So I was stateless.

When I tried to plead with the government that I needed to go and see my parents as my father was seriously ill. The minister responsible replied:

Although it is to your credit that you notified the Immigration and Nationality Directorate of the circumstances of your entry to the United Kingdom, it has taken over twenty five years for you to do so. While I accept that you, as a twelve year old, would not have been aware of the illegality of your entry to the United Kingdom at that time, I am satisfied that you were fully aware of the deception during the majority of your adult years in the United Kingdom and your breach of the immigration laws can only be classed as deliberate.

While I was waiting to get my nationality, I could not go out of the country. It had been quite a few years since I had seen my parents. Fortunately, as well as writing letters, now I was able to phone them. Modern technology had come to our village. I would phone the GPO in the local bazaar. They would send someone to fetch my parents. A few minutes later I would phone again and they would be there. Of course, on rare occasions, I would phone the second time only to be told my parents were not home. I would ask the GPO to let my folks know that I had called. For them, next best thing to speaking to me was knowing that I had phoned.

A number of people wrote to the government on my behalf at this point:

Letter 1

After much reflection K decided to enter into a personal relationship with God. This has expressed itself in Baptism. As his faith has matured so has his desire towards anyone that he becomes involved in; he acts wisely and seeks their best interests and development of character and spirituality. As a result of their leadership, K and his wife are considered pillars of the church.

It was with much heart searching that he took his decision to inform you of his immigration circumstances. This is a reflection of his faith and desire to be a speaker of truth in the expression of his life to everyone.

We fully support his action and would ask you to look favourably on his request and grant him citizenship in his true name and identity.

Letter 2

I am writing to express my dismay at the decision not to grant K naturalisation as a British citizen.

I have known him for over 5 years and I regard him as a citizen who is making an enormous contribution to the life of this city and its different communities. I find it astonishing, given his frankness and integrity that his application should not be considered favourable, and I wish to register my protest. I am sending a copy of this letter to Mr O'Brien

(Member of Parliament and Minister for Immigration) *as it seems to me that if a civilised country cannot entertain an application in these circumstances, we are in serious trouble. . . . . The explanation that K has been given as to why he could not be granted naturalisation I think is totally inadequate, given the circumstances of the case and I look forward to hearing from you at your earliest convenience.*

Letter 3

K has contributed a great deal to our society, as a bringer-together of people in this neighbourhood, in his church and in his employment as youth worker, FE teacher and as an educational administrator.

As a British-born national I wholeheartedly support K's appeal for British nationality. It would be a sad reflection on British Administration if the application was to fail because the letter of the law overrides the spirit of integrity demonstrated by this case.

Ps A copy of this letter and background information has been sent to the Archbishop of Canterbury, Dr George Carey.

It was probably one of the few occasions when I wished that I had a different skin colour. Perhaps, then, like Zola Budd, my application for citizenship would have taken less time.

Overall, it took nearly four years to convince the British government of why I had come forward now and not before to tell them about my immigration situation. For me, my British passport is a very special document. If we ever write down what it means to be British, I would certainly wish to include truth and integrity in the values which define our society.

It amused me and those around me to know that the Hinduja Brothers Passport Affair was going on during this period. While I was struggling to convince the British government of my case following Biblical teaching in our supposedly Christian country, here was a family who were buying their way into our country's nationality. The same government ministers, while refusing my application, were letting things go through on the nod. There was me thinking that this kind of practice happened elsewhere. As they say, for every rule there is an exception! Money may not be able to buy you love but it could buy you a passport, even here in a country which prides itself on the rule of law and equality for all.

It was now a few years into my Christian life. The school where I worked merged with another school due to falling rolls. Across the two schools, those of us in managerial positions—I was a head of department—had to re-apply for our own jobs since they did not need two sets of managers. I was unsuccessful in getting one of the jobs. Now I was faced with a choice. It was either take a post at a lower level or accept redundancy and leave.

This was a major decision for me. I had never been unemployed nor claimed social security benefits from the government, except during university holidays. This was no mean achievement, given the popular stereotype of Pakistanis scrounging off the government. So, I began to think about what was the right decision to take.

According to the Christian teaching I had begun to receive, I knew that, unlike before, I could pray about making such a big decision. I could seek guidance from the Lord. I wondered how this would work out. Would God suddenly appear and say, "Don't be foolish and take redundancy," or "Take redundancy because I have plans for you to do something else."?

I set out systematically to speak to a range of people in my network, not all of whom were Christian. I found that some of the best input came from friends who were not in my line of work. They raised fresh perspectives and questions, which only an 'outsider' could do. I must have had nearly twenty conversations. Throughout the process, fellow Christians were praying for me and asking God to clarify my decision-making. On one occasion I was given Psalm 34, on another occasion Psalm 16. And on yet another occasion I was given Psalm 23. I read them from time to time to remind myself of what is said in them. In particular, I read the last one:

> *The LORD is my shepherd, I lack nothing.*
> *He makes me lie down in green pastures,*
> *he leads me beside quiet waters,*
> *he refreshes my soul.*
> *He guides me along the right paths for his name's sake.*
> *Even though I walk through the darkest valley,*
> *I will fear no evil, for you are with me;*
> *your rod and your staff, they comfort me.*
>
> *You prepare a table before me in the presence of my enemies.*
> *You anoint my head with oil; my cup overflows.*

Surely your goodness and love will follow me all the days of my life,
and I will dwell in the house of the LORD forever.

After a couple of months, one of my Christian brothers said to me, "Listen to your heart; God will put in your heart what He wants you to do."

While I did not want to accept a lower position, I knew it was risky to leave given that I had to support a family in England and parents in Pakistan. However, after further prayer and reflection, I felt God was saying, "Leave, take redundancy. I will provide for you." So I left.

At the time of writing it has been eleven years since that date. With confidence, I can say that it has been the best eleven years of my life. He has provided work for me, satisfying and well-paid work, opportunities to grow and develop and in the process has transformed me into a new person.

I am yet again facing a redundancy situation. Going through this one seems so much easier, not only because I am doing it in God's strength but also because I have a strengthened faith; knowing that the last decade has been the best years of my life which I would have missed had I not listened to God. It also helps me to reassure my colleagues who are also facing the situation with me. I wish I could say to them "Trust the Lord" but in the secular world we live in, it would not be a good idea to mention God.

Soon after taking redundancy, I took a day out of my schedule to go on a 'retreat.' There were a number of us there but, unlike group or organised retreats, beyond eating together we spent time on our own, listening to God. He spoke to me through one of the organisers and pointed out that I would have a prosperous future. He also gave me plenty of rest and peace.

It was a very pleasant spring day. The centre was in the open Shropshire countryside. There was a moment in the day when I was outside. I could smell the countryside and get drunk on its natural beauty. Smoke was coming out of one of the farms some distance away. Although, it was the afternoon, I suddenly heard a cockerel crowing, just like they used to in my village. It suddenly felt as if the Lord was saying, "My dear son, I am well pleased with you. I know, because of your passport, you cannot go to the village of your birth so I have brought it here for you." The only thing that was missing was my mother's voice calling me from somewhere in our fields, as she used to.

My search for parents, especially a father figure, had finally come to an end. I had reached my destination. I was the little boy who had managed to reach the source of the rainbow and find his gold. I had found my Father. I had also found a whole group of people who would provide an extended family environment for my children, similar to the one I was surrounded with as a child.

Telling the truth, again

A few years later, I had an opportunity to experience the immigration system a second time. This time, I had applied for a visitor's visa for my mother so she could come and see her grandchildren. The application was refused on the grounds that she would come to England for a few months but then refuse to go back as many Pakistani elderly people in her position were doing. The truth was we had no intention of wanting her to over-stay and she had no such intention either. But it was a different matter altogether to persuade the authorities.

The letter from the immigration authorities read:

> Although the Appellant (my mother) *claimed she wished to visit the United Kingdom for six months, the Entry Clearance Officer found that the Appellant had failed to show sufficiently strong family, social or economic ties to Pakistan to satisfy him on the balance of probabilities that she intended to leave the United Kingdom on completion of her short visit.*

In this kind of situation, it would be normal for someone from my community to come up with some tale of woe in order to strengthen our case. I was advised by some in my family to get a letter from a doctor to show that someone in our family was seriously ill thus needing my mother to come as a matter of urgency.

The old 'me' might have gone along with such a ploy but the new 'me' wished to do it differently. I could not bring myself to be a part of any such deception. So, off I went to appear in front of the immigration appeal judge. She was taken aback when I said that I could understand how things looked from their perspective. I then set out to explain why it was unlikely for my mother to over-stay her visit.

I was equipped with one thing and one thing only: truth. I explained the kind of life my mother was used to in rural Kashmir with a 100% Muslim population in comparison to our very different lifestyle as a Christian, middle class, professional family.

Telling the truth worked. I did not have to embroider the case to suit the situation. A few weeks after my appearance in front of the immigration judge, I received a letter from them. It informed me that, yes, my mother can come to visit us. Their position was outlined in a four page letter which included the following key paragraph:

> I find the sponsor entirely credible and although he can only give limited evidence as to the Appellant's intention to return to Pakistan I find that after hearing evidence of the Appellant's lifestyle in Pakistan I am satisfied to the required standard that she does not have any intention to stay in the United Kingdom after the expiry of her entry clearance. In any event I am satisfied that the sponsor would not be in a position to look after the Appellant in the United Kingdom given the sponsor's lifestyle. I find that this is a genuine application for a short family visit and I allow this appeal.

So, telling the truth worked a second time. My dear mother came. She had a great time with us as well as seeing all the extended family. I discovered that she likes to listen to music so I was able to share my Bruce Springsteen DVD with her. One Sunday morning, when I told her what we do normally at that time, she gave me permission to go to church. This meant a great deal to me. And, at the end of her entry clearance, as promised, she returned to the world she calls home.

At times it felt as if making some of the big decisions according to Christian teaching were a lot easier; it was more of a challenge dealing with the more personal, day-to-day stuff. One of the things I am still working on is to say sorry. Not just a quick 'I'm sorry' and then move on as if nothing had happened, but actually asking for forgiveness at a deeper and more honest level.

Another personal area I had to address was not to swear. Although I was not the swearing kind, I still needed to remind myself that every time I uttered a profanity, it was dirtying my mouth. It was the same mouth that I would be using to praise God. So now I try to swear a little less and say sorry a little more.

When I first decided to follow Christ, it was purely on the basis of what I observed in the behaviour of Christians. I had not obtained any objective evidence that there was a God who was a part of a Trinity which included Jesus Christ and the Holy Spirit. My Christian faith and relationship with God finds its meaning when I glance back at the transformation which has taken place over the past sixteen years. I wish I could respond to my colleague who had, in his long letter to me in my early days as a Christian, talked about "faith without evidence." I would tell him that my faith was no "myth" or "fantasy." I would simply point to him all that God has done in my life during the fifteen years since. Similarly, if I was to answer the question on the Alpha Course leaflet, "Does God exist? Yes □, No □, or Probably □," I would want to add my own, fourth option: DEFINITELY. I may not be David or Gideon, but with His strength I can defeat Goliath and the Midianites.

Dear reader,

Thank you for taking the trouble to read my book. It began life as a note to my fellow Christians who plod on, day in day out, sharing the gospel and often without much to show for their efforts. I wanted to encourage them to hang on in there because occasionally, just occasionally, you'll see the fruit. But, as I began to write, I decided to take the opportunity to tell the story of my community in relation to England. At this point I realised that there would be much a Christian might understand but it would be meaningless to someone back in my village who might be reading my book, in English, Urdu or listening to it in Pahari. He is not likely to know his Alpha from his Cross. So I decided I had better explain everything. Consequently, I am sorry to those of you who knew about such things. I hope you found my own take on them worth reading.

My story continues. For now, I would like to conclude it with the words of the hymn *I will bless the Lord forever*. It sums up my position and the agenda for the remainder of my life:

I will trust Him at all times. He has delivered me from all fear; And He has set my feet upon a rock.

I'll say of the Lord: You are my shield, my strength, my portion
Deliverer, my shelter, strong tower, my very present help in time of need.

Whom have I in heaven but You. There's none I desire beside You

It seems a long time since the day I was given those words from Jeremiah.
I feel the Lord is saying to me now:

You are my servant, whom I uphold, my chosen one, in whom I delight.
I will put my Spirit on you and you will bring justice to the nations.
You will not shout or cry out or raise your voice in the streets. A bruised
reed you will not break and a smouldering wick you will not snuff out.
In faithfulness, you will bring forth justice; you will not falter or be
discouraged till you establish justice on earth. In your law the islands
will put their hope.

This is what I the Lord say to you: I who created the heavens and
stretched them out, who spread the earth and all that comes out of it,
who gives breath to its people and life to those who walk in it: I, the
Lord, have called you in righteousness; I will take hold of your hand.
I will keep you and will make you to be a covenant for the people and
a light for the Gentiles, to open eyes that are blind, to free captives
from prison and to release from the dungeon those who sit in darkness.
(Isaiah 42)

To paraphrase Amos, I was neither a prophet nor the son of a prophet.
I was a village boy who grew up in a world which did not have modern
facilities and whose idea of a toilet was the nearest field. Where he
worked, my father was in the most menial job possible. Like Amos, I
also took care of goats and buffalos. I spoke a language which did not
even have a name. Later, when I arrived in England, to many around me
I was just another 'Paki' who could not speak proper English and who
came from a community which was despised then and has continued to
be so.

Forty-two years on, now that I have learnt sufficient English and a little
more besides, I wonder what the Lord has in mind for me for the rest of
my life in this world. Like the little boy, holding tightly onto my Father's
hand; as one with my Instructor and with my earpiece connected to my
Producer, I am ready to go on this adventure.